The Mental Keys to Hitting

The Mental Keys to Hitting
A Handbook of Strategies for
Performance Enhancement

By
H. A. Dorfman

Guilford, Connecticut

An imprint of Globe Pequot
Trade Division of The Rowman & Littlefield Publishing Group, Inc.
4501 Forbes Boulevard, Suite 200, Lanham, Maryland 20706

Distributed by NATIONAL BOOK NETWORK
800-462-6420

British Library Cataloguing-in-Publication Information Available

Library of Congress Cataloging-in-Publication Data Available
ISBN 978-1-63076-186-8 (paperback)
ISBN 978-1-63076-187-5 (e-book)

∞™ The paper used in this publication meets the minimum requirements of American National Standard for Information Sciences—Permanence of Paper for Printed Library Materials, ANSI/NISO Z39.48-1992.

Printed in the United States of America

Contents

ABOUT THE AUTHOR ix

FOREWORD xi

INTRODUCTION xvii

CHAPTER 1
First and Foremost, SEE THE BALL! 1

CHAPTER 2
Aggressiveness under Control 7

CHAPTER 3
Setting Your Goals vs. Living Others' Expectations 18

CHAPTER 4
Self-Coaching: Making Adjustments
in the Heat of the Battle..26

CHAPTER 5
Self-Talk (Talk Right; Walk Right) 32

CHAPTER 6
Paying Proper Attention: The Ability to
Concentrate on Task...40

CHAPTER 7
Perspective: Recognizing the Real 50

CHAPTER 8
Routine, Ritual, and Superstition: Who's in Control?............61

CHAPTER 9
The Preparation Cycle 66

CHAPTER 10
Relax the Mind: Relax the Muscles 74

CHAPTER 11
Approach, Result, Response:
Knowing What Can and Cannot Be Controlled 82

CHAPTER 12
Confidence and Capacity 89

CHAPTER 13
After-words...95

For Anita, Melissa, and Dan:
The top of my batting order.

Some of the material in this book previously appeared in:

@ THE PLATE, a newsletter,
published by MasterPlan Sports & Fitness

&

PRO, a magazine distributed to professional athletes,
published by Street & Smith.

About the Author

Harvey A. Dorfman was a noted sports psychologist as well as a sports psychology counselor with the Scott Boras Agency. He began his career in baseball psychology with the Oakland Athletics as their full-time instructor and counselor. He later worked with the Florida Marlins and Tampa Bay Devil Rays in a similar capacity before joining the Scott Boras Agency. Recognized as a leading sports psychologist across the world, Dorfman was also a columnist and freelance journalist with articles appearing in *The New York Times*, *The Boston Globe*, and *The Miami Herald*. During his career, he lectured extensively on sports psychology, management and leadership training, and personal development as well as provided counseling services to professional teams in the NHL. He was the author of three other books: *Coaching the Mental Game*, *The Mental Game of Baseball*, and *The Mental ABCs of Pitching*.

Foreword

IN APPRECIATION OF HARVEY DORFMAN
By Rick Wolff

When Harvey Dorfman passed away in 2011 at the age of 75, major league baseball lost one of its all-time greats.

Over the last 30 years, just about every major league player, general manager, field manager, and agent either knew Harvey or certainly had heard of his impact. They all knew of the mental magic he worked on talented ballplayers.

Harvey was indeed a singular individual, certainly one of a kind.

So . . . who was Harvey Dorfman?

In short, he introduced the world of major league baseball to the wonders of sports psychology. And he did it in a most unique and unusual way.

You know the old Yogi Berra expression that "half of this game is 90 percent mental"? I don't know if Dorfman ever met Yogi, but trust me on this: Harvey certainly agreed with Yogi. Baseball, which is a game based upon constant failure and daily disappointment, is pockmarked by all sorts of mental distractions, obsessions, anxieties, and even superstitions. Harvey knew all of this, inhaled it all, and helped pro players of all stripes come to terms with their fears.

A man of apparent contradictions, Harvey was a most educated and literate gentleman. He was a man of letters, a true scholar. Yet to better communicate with ballplayers, he could swear like a drunken sailor with enough profanity mixed in to peel paint off a wall. Harvey offered no apology for this approach; he just knew that ballplayers would feel more comfortable with him if he spoke the language of dugouts.

But Harvey was indeed a lifelong lover of books. When I first met him and his lovely wife, Anita, at their home in Prescott, Arizona, an entire side of their living room wall was stacked from floor to ceiling with books and more books.

Originally trained as a high school English teacher, Dorfman consumed the *New York Times Book Review* each week in much the same way he would go over the daily baseball box scores.

Back in the 1970s Harvey, Anita, and their two kids resided in Vermont, where Dorfman taught in a small private school and wrote newspaper columns. He was very proud that he coached the school's girls' basketball team to great success. But during the summer months Dorfman would attend Vermont Expos minor league games, and it was there that he befriended Karl Kuehl, who oversaw the Expos minor league system.

Over the course of that summer, Kuehl became so impressed with Dorfman's approach to baseball that when Kuehl left the Expos to join the Oakland Athletics, he made sure to hire Harvey as a kind of mental skills coach.

This was a totally new concept. Understand that this was unprecedented in organized baseball. For example, when I was playing in the Detroit Tigers organization in the early 1970s, after having studied psychology as an undergraduate at Harvard, the prevailing attitude in pro baseball was that "any player who needs to talk to a shrink needs to have his head examined."

As such, when Dorfman was hired by Oakland, this was a monumental breakthrough for sports psychology. But in truth, Harvey was never trained as a psychologist; he was a schoolteacher and coach. He never had a doctorate in psychology.

But he possessed one amazing skill: He knew how to communicate with ballplayers. He knew how to get them to open up about their fears, worries, and insecurities.

And then, once the superstar millionaire ballplayer would confide in Harvey about his batting slump or how he can't throw strikes any more, Harvey would actively listen. But he didn't offer sympathy or offer a kindly smile.

Rather, just the opposite. Harv would roar at the player and demand in a loud voice: "Okay, hot shot, you're hitting under the Mendoza line. . . . Tell me—what are you going to do about it? *How are you going to make the appropriate adjustments?*"

In other words, Harvey was very big on getting players to confront their shortcomings and failings. Harvey would often tell me that he saw his job to "hold a mirror to these guys" so they could deal with their issues. "Hey," Harvey would bark at me, "somebody has to tell these guys the truth! *That's my job!*"

Trust me, Harvey was not big on telling major leaguers to "just take a deep breath" or to "just think positive thoughts." Harvey didn't put any stock in those approaches. Ironically, these days it seems that lots of sports psychologists who work for major league teams do offer that kind of Pollyanna advice. Harvey would scoff, "Don't give me any of that hold hands and sing Kumbaya BS! That's not going to get you to hit better!"

Harvey once told me that he felt that too many stars today are surrounded by so many sycophants and "yes-men" that very few of these players ever hear the truth. Dorfman saw his role as providing a sharp contrast—being the loud voice of reality. And once the player heard what Dorfman was saying, he would begin to get a sense of what was holding him back. That was the key.

Take Jamie Moyer. The oldest pitcher to ever win a game in the big leagues at age 49, Moyer writes in his autobiography, *Just Tell Me I Can't,* that he owes his entire major league career to Dorfman. If you recall, Moyer didn't throw hard enough to break a pane of glass. But he pitched in the bigs for 25 years and came close to winning 300 games.

As is written on the cover of his book: "Moyer was just about finished as a big leaguer at 29 until he fatefully encountered a gravel-voiced, highly confrontational mental skills coach named Harvey Dorfman. Listening to the 'in-your-face' provocations of Dorfman, Moyer began to re-invent and re-construct his mental approach to the game."

But there were a lot more followers than just Jamie Moyer. Dozens more. I once visited Harvey's home when he moved to North Carolina later in his life. His office walls were covered with personally autographed photos of major league stars, all with inscriptions like: "Harvey—I owe my career to you" or "If you weren't for you, Harv, I wouldn't still be in the big leagues."

The list of players who sought out Dorfman? Names like Roy Halladay . . . Brad Lidge . . . Greg Maddux . . . Jim Abbott . . . Al Leiter . . . Kevin Brown . . . Mike Pelfrey . . . Rick Ankiel

. . . Bob Welch . . . and on and on. All sorts of big name stars, all of whom had worked with and listened to Harvey.

Harvey would always blush when the top players referred to him as "baseball's best kept secret." They would lovingly refer to him as "baseball's shrink." But Harvey would laugh in protest and say, "I'm not a *shrink*. . . . I'm a *stretch!* I'm trying to get these guys to *stretch* their minds!"

The year was 1989. The phone rang in my Manhattan office, and a man I didn't know was telling me how much he enjoyed my book *The Psychology of Winning Baseball*. He said he knew I had played pro ball and had studied psychology. Flattered by such an unexpected call, I was eager to get the caller's name.

He said his name was Harvey Dorfman.

But there was more. Harvey explained that he worked for the Oakland Athletics as their sports psychology coach, and that he was always being approached by other major league teams to jump ship to their club. He said he was very happy working for Oakland and asked whether it would be okay if he gave my name to other major league teams if they were looking for a sports psychology coach.

"Sure, that's more than fine with me," I told Harvey. I was very flattered. But deep down, I really didn't expect much to happen.

But something did happen. Within the next few days, I started to receive phone calls from no fewer than six major league general managers. Hank Peters of the Indians; Roland Hemond from the Orioles; Jerry Reinsdorf, the owner of the White Sox; and so forth. They were all calling me at the suggestion of Harvey Dorfman.

Suddenly I found myself being courted like a college recruit as each GM was offering me a deal to come and work with their players. I ended up signing with the Indians because I was impressed with Hank Peters and his soon-to-become successor John Hart. A young Dan O'Dowd was Hart's assistant. (Dan went onto become the GM of the Rockies). Plus the Indians had some young, talented kids in their minor league system like Jim Thome, Manny Ramirez, Albert Belle, Charlie Nagy, and so on.

In short, solely thanks to Harvey—a man I had never met—I got the chance of a lifetime to work for a number of years with the Cleveland Indians at the highest levels as their roving sports psychology coach. I even received a 1995 American League championship ring for efforts with the Tribe.

Here's the bottom line: As of today there's no wing in the Hall of Fame for sports psychology, but clearly if there were one, Harvey Dorfman would be a first-ballot unanimous choice. He was absolutely unique. And the best news is that his legacy lives on with his extraordinarily well-written books on the mental side of baseball.

For years, aspiring ballplayers have devoured Harvey's books. They have become de facto mandatory reading at all levels of the game.

So consider yourself lucky. You're about to turn the page and learn from the master. . . . Harvey Dorfman.

Rick Wolff is one of the nation's leading experts on sports psychology and is the longtime host of "The Sports Edge" on WFAN Radio in New York City. Drafted by the Detroit Tigers after his junior year at Harvard, Wolff played two years in the minors before going on to a career in coaching, sports psychology, publishing, and sports commentary. You can read more about him at askcoachwolff.com.

INTRODUCTION

It probably isn't appropriate to call *The Mental Keys to Hitting* the third book of a "trilogy." Yet that's the way it has been considered by those who encouraged the writing of it. Following *The Mental Game of Baseball* and *The Mental ABC's of Pitching,* this work does complete, for me, an instructional series based on intellectual and psychological approaches and strategies for playing the game of baseball at the highest level, talent notwithstanding.

Players' talents are based on genetic gifts. In that sense, they are essentially predisposed to be as good as they were fated to be. Players' attitudes, perspectives, approaches and responses are based on choices they make. In that regard, they are capable of being as good as they choose to be.

Players make choices, often without realizing they're doing so. To allow a poor approach to be repeated over and over again—one which greatly inhibits effective performance—is to make a choice, whether it is a conscious one or an unconscious one. For example, a hitter who is confused and frustrated brings the response to his at-bats. He chooses to dwell on the problem, rather than the solution. Self-pity or anger leads to a loss of confidence. Loss of confidence further distracts him. His distraction gets in the way of his ability to see the ball well. The proverbial snowball effect has taken over. So much for having a good day at the plate.

The player's choice has been to operate out of his emotional system instead of his rational system. It's understandable, but unacceptable nevertheless.

And so, players—hitters, in this context—must learn to harness their emotions and choose to think appropriately before they act. Before they hit. And, actually, after they've hit, as well. The before and after are the approaches and responses that I constantly talk about with players. They should be simple and clear to the hitter. They should and will preempt "worries" about the expectations of others, about results, about any external distraction.

An enhanced performance for a hitter starts with thinking and acting effectively. His feelings are impediments, not enhancers. This manual will help the hitter to identify the difference—and to apply what he understands to his game.

Players often complain to me that "the game is complicated." I tell them that the game is simple. People are complicated. "Have a plan, relax, see the ball and trust your muscles." Keep it simple, I tell them. That's the challenge. And that is what every exceptional athlete learns to do. Not always, but usually. Using mental discipline, he applies that "simplistic" information to his game. His consistent behavior leads to consistent performance.

The Mental Keys to Hitting provides that requisite information and helps guide hitters (and coaches) in their quest to improve mental approaches to hitting. Players and coaches work long and hard on the mechanics of hitting. But proper "mental mechanics" are as essential as the physical. Of course, some would say more essential. It requires hard work—dedication. An "ordeal," I call it. The price of success is perseverance. The initial cost of failure is considerably less. Phil Nevin—and many others—have learned that.

When Karl Kuehl, co-author of *The Mental Game of Baseball,* was coaching with the Minnesota Twins in the 1980s, his most precocious student of the mental aspects of baseball was outfielder Gary Ward. More recently, Gary's son, Daryle won the Houston Astros "top rookie" award - in 1999. Explaining his success, the 23-year-old said, "My dad helped me with the mental part of the game. I think that's 90 percent of hitting."

Whatever the percentage may be, the importance of "the mental game" is universally agreed upon. But it must be practiced diligently and effectively. It's my hope that this book will encourage and enable hitters and coaches to do so.

I always tell players that they must know what to do on and off the field. With that in mind, I have included, at the end of each chapter, a list of essential mental keys that will help remind a hitter of what, specifically, he should be doing "above the shoulders." Much of it can also be applied to one's life out of a baseball uniform.

The concluding "chapter" in this book is titled *After-words.* It is a "mouthful" ("headful"?) of words and phrases (listed alphabetically) that hitters have most frequently asked me about over the years. Or terms that I've heard them talking about. In the chapter, I provide my own interpretation, definition, and commentary, as I've provided them to the hitters. Some topics are more developed than others, of course, according to the degree of concern expressed to me by hitters—and the significance I've arbitrarily given to the topics.

The book which I co-authored with Karl Kuehl, *The Mental Game of Baseball,* has an expansive scope, whereas this work, in my estimation, is a very basic "handbook"—specific to hitting. Those who may also wish a more comprehensive treatment of the "mental game" can refer to that work, as well, if they haven't already.

Finally, it should be made clear that many ideas, suggestions, and keys are repeated and cross-referenced throughout the book. They are conscious reiterations, not careless redundancies. We all need repetition to assist us in our quest for growth and mastery. Muscular and mental.

As a case in point, a significant number of major league players have asked me, in frustration with themselves, "How many times are you going to have to tell me the same thing?" My answer: "As many times as I have to." Until it's in there. Until it's secured at the highest level of consciousness.

There are many externals that are capable of dislodging learning. The more you read and hear the things you should want to do, the more likely you'll develop and retain a thoughtful, clear, and incorruptible understanding. Then, "all" that remains is to do it. Over and over again. Such efficacy keeps athletes—hitters—consistently near their peak and very often at it.

-H.A. Dorfman, 2001

"[Jose] Cruz is a guy who has to work on the mental part of hitting... That's half the battle."
—Cito Gaston, Toronto hitting coach
2000

"I was so stupid. I did so many immature things. I was a miserable person to be around. It was like the mental side, the psychological side of baseball didn't exist for me. I figured I'd just get by on the same talent."
—Phil Nevin, San Diego Padres third baseman
2000

"You need to play this game with a mental capacity that's mature and patient...Sometimes a youthful, strong kid can't play the game above the shoulders. This is a game you can play with bad body parts and still be successful. I think that's been a pure key to my success."
—Jeff Kent, San Francisco Giants second baseman
National League MVP
2000

"The highest reward for a person's toil is not what they get for it, but what they become by it."
—John Ruskin, English writer/sociologist
1859

#1 See The Ball!

CHAPTER 1

First and Foremost,
SEE THE BALL!

"Vision is the art of seeing things invisible."
— Jonathan Swift, *Thoughts on Various Subjects*

Well, let's start by saying a baseball thrown by a pitcher to a batter certainly *is* "visible." But seeing it well and reacting to it effectively, having a clear mind, so as to *keep it from being "invisible"* — which is the hitter's objective — is certainly one of the most formidable tasks in sport. That is the hitter's objective and doing it well is artful enough for him.

Consider this: A baseball bat at its widest is three and three-quarters inches in diameter. A ball comes toward the hitter at the speed of 80 to 90-plus miles an hour. A 90-mile-an-hour fastball reaches the plate in four-tenths of a second. The hitter has just about one-tenth of a second to pick up the ball.

In dealing with the mental approach to hitting, a player must establish his priority — his core understanding of what's *at the top of the list* of requirements for being a skilled hitter. I've told countless professional players, "However good your mechanics may be, you won't succeed if I blindfold you." First things first: see the ball! "Track it and whack it," as I have often shouted from the dugout.

Vision itself may be a physiological issue, but *what* we look at and *how* we look at it is affected by our mental state. What is

1

"going on" internally affects our ability to properly see and interpret the external world. And a hitter's physical behavior will thereby be affected.

Our problems are as individual as our perceptions. On the same day during a spring training session years ago, I had three big league players tell me they had trouble seeing the ball. They shared the same symptom, but they each had a unique problem. The first, it turned out, needed corrective lenses. So that was a physiological issue.

The second player was preoccupied with an agonizing family problem. He couldn't get it out of his mind. His concentration on the field suffered, of course. He didn't realize how much that affected his ability to focus on task. The task, as a hitter, of seeing the ball.

The third player had no idea how to find the pitcher's release point unless he was facing a pitcher who threw "over the top" — straight overhand. Each player was adversely affected in the batter's box by his individual need. But the universal need of every hitter is to see the ball well.

Before looking for answers to a hitting problem elsewhere, the player should first ask himself this question: "Am I seeing the ball well?" If the answer is that he's not, then he must ask, "Why not?" Too often, a hitter who is struggling makes immediate changes to his mechanics — to his physical approach. This compounds the difficulty. Kinetic memory — muscle memory — allows a player to have a consistent mechanical approach — unless the player inhibits his muscles by thinking too much. He gets in the way of his natural, physical function. He begins to be what I call a self-conscious hitter, thinking about all manner of things which distract him while in the box. He's got everything on his mind. *Everything except the ball!*

During the 2000 season, Jose Canseco was in a bad hitting slump before going on the disabled list. Readying himself to come off the D.L. he took extra batting practice — not working on physical mechanics, but rather on seeing the ball well and not jumping at so many pitches. [See Chapter 2]

It's hard to remember that this elemental skill is not only

prerequisite to being a good hitter, but without it all other skills are negated. The ability to simplify is the ability to eliminate the unnecessary so that the necessary may express itself. Focusing on the ball is simply necessary.

Item: Shortstop Alex Rodriguez hit .308 in August 2000. It had been his "worst" month of the season. Early in September, A-Rod said that things were going better at the plate. The reason? "I've been seeing the ball the last couple of weeks."

The Cardinals' pitcher Rick Ankiel is also a very respectable hitter. His hitting .462 with two home runs and a triple in his first 12 at-bats in his rookie season prompted the team's hitting coach, Mike Easler, to say, "He doesn't know what he's doing; he's just talented. There's no mechanics, no technique." Better stated, there's no pre-occupation with mechanics. The mechanics are a product of natural talent, which is true of the vast majority of hitters. "I don't worry about that stuff," Ankiel explained to me. "I just look for the ball and hit it."

In a nationally published magazine article last year, catcher Terry Steinbach gave an interviewer a sample of a conversation he would have with me when he was struggling at the plate. Steinbach said that however he would start the talk, or perceive the problem, the answer always seemed to come only after I asked him, "Are you seeing the ball?" Steinbach would most often and most emphatically respond, "Sure, yeah, I am." And I wouldn't accept his answer. After getting through the maze of what his initial complaints and perceptions were, he'd realize he hadn't been tracking it.

Years ago, Harold Baines, already a veteran player, and an acknowledged consistent hitter, was struggling. He told me he "wasn't comfortable" at the plate. Many people had tried to help him by giving him advice about where to stand in the box, how to hold his hands, and so on. It hurt more than it helped, because he changed his previously consistent focus.

We had breakfast in our Minnesota hotel the next morning. I asked him how many times he'd hit well when he hadn't felt "comfortable." He responded, "Many times." I then asked him how many times he had good days when he didn't see the ball well. "Never," he said. That night he regained his approach, after using his first at-bat just to track the ball. He saw five pitches and was called out on strikes. But he was reassured by his ability to track the ball. For the rest of the game he tracked it — and whacked it. (Home run, double, line drive out.)

After the game, he told me he was "embarrassed" that at this stage of his career he still had to be reminded to see the ball. "Almost everyone needs reminding," I told him. Apparently, he remembered very well for the number of years in his career that followed.

Hitters take for granted that they *see* the ball, but they don't make the distinction between a casual, fuzzy focus and one that is intense and sharp. Just as we can hear without concentrated *listening*, we can see without having a concentrated clarity. No one kept it simple as well as Pete Rose. He admitted to not being "a rocket scientist," but he knew instinctively that rocket scientists wouldn't be good hitters. They would think too deeply and too much, and their attention would be divided during their at-bats. Thoughts about rocketry and hitting don't get along well in the batter's box. It divides the hitter's attention and decreases the size of the ball proportionate to the attention given to anything *but* the ball.

In 2000, Toronto's Carlos Delgado certainly "put up the numbers" that players covet. His explanation: "I can see the ball better. I've been trying to do that for years… Pitches seem slower to me...All I want to do is just give myself a chance to see the ball early..." [There's a bit more to it. See Chapter 2.]

ESPN's Dan Patrick asked Future Hall-of-Famer Barry Bonds, "What's the best swing in baseball?" Bonds simple response, "The contact one." The prerequisite? See the ball, and trust your muscles. They'll give you the swing you want. And *then* good, hard contact.

Hitters who are thinking about their mechanics — or anything else — during their at-bats are no better off than the hypothetical scientists referred to earlier. Such players become mechanical scientists, not effective batsmen. They forget what Ralph Waldo Emerson knew — and he wasn't even a hitter. "The eye," he wrote, "obeys exactly the action of the mind."

Want to see the ball better? *Think ball!*

 **REMEMBER**

• Whether struggling or doing well, give yourself regular "reality checks" related to how well you're seeing the ball. Grade yourself after each at-bat, in terms of how well you saw the ball — tracked the ball. "Was that my best look? Was it a Number 1 look (best), a Number 2 ...?" And so on. Using this procedure, you'll keep the level of awareness high and not allow yourself a prolonged period of not being attentive to the ball.

• When you are not having good looks, use your next at-bat to establish your concentration on the ball. Take the first pitch and *track it all the way* to the catcher's mitt. You know it's going to be a "take," so you have no other obligation than to see the ball. Having done that, you discipline your mind and eyes. Step out of the box and tell yourself to "look for the ball and be easy." React to the pitch as you see it with a swing or take.

• The deeper you can get into the count, the better. You'll see more pitches and help yourself as a result. This, of course, can more easily be accomplished if you get ahead in the count immediately, or are willing (according to the circumstance of the game) to use the entire at-bat, à la Baines. Use every at-bat to your purpose, instead of allowing it use you.

• Before each at-bat — before you get in the box — coach yourself. Remind yourself by repeating the mantra, "See the ball; be easy." It's simple to say, harder to do. It requires *discipline* and *trust* (to be discussed in later chapters), the traits of great hitters. Habit is a practice long pursued. Cultivate the good habit of seeing that ball. Then, put a hurt on it.

CHAPTER 2

Aggressiveness under Control

"You've got to have the mentality that you are going to make somebody pay when you're at bat."
— Mo Vaughn, Angels first baseman, 2000

"[Troy Glaus] has a good eye now, but sometimes gets himself in trouble by taking too many strikes. I guess you could call it 'too disciplined.'"
— Mickey Hatcher, Angels hitting coach, 2000

The Greeks had something to offer hitters. "Nothing in excess," they said. And I pass that philosophy on to the hitters I work with. Mental balance, I call it. The idea is applied to a hitting philosophy as "aggressiveness under control." One without the other leads to undesirable consequences. Finding the right balance for each individual is the ideal.

Every car has an accelerator and a brake. The accelerator represents aggressiveness — helping you to get where you're going. The brake represents control — assuring that when you get there, you're in one piece. Gas pedal and brake are necessary to appropriate operation of the vehicle, as both aggressiveness and control are essential to successful hitting. That is the philosophy I advocate.

NHL goalie Ed Belfour enjoys speed. He acknowledges this clearly in a TV commercial, during which he takes an amusement park ride and shouts, "Faster! Faster!" The security guards who accompany him are frozen in terror. But Belfour knows better when he's in his racing cars and when he's in the nets. "When you're racing, you have to stay real focused…and you have to stay calm. When you get that adrenaline flowing in a race car, you've got to stay in control — a lot like playing in goal." And like being in the batter's box.

The phrase "aggressiveness under control" is more appropriate than "controlled aggressiveness" as a credo for hitters. Colorado's Todd Helton has done pretty well for himself, though he's used the latter phrase. But I still recommend "aggressiveness" as the operative word.

The Oakland A's still teach the balance throughout their entire system, as they did when I was working there between 1984 and 1993. In 2000, General Manager Billy Beane watched the organization's Triple-A Sacramento team clinch the Pacific Coast League title with a 15-4 victory. Said Beane, "They hit five home runs and walked ten times. It was beautiful." It's been called Oakland's "walking and whacking" philosophy. I'd say "whacking and walking." Beane did, in fact, mention the homers first, rather than the bases on balls.

I tell hitters that they start a car's movement by using the gas pedal first. That's aggressiveness. A hitter's first thought before going to the plate should be about making good, solid contact. He anticipates a pitch he can hit and is ready for it when he sees it. He does not anticipate taking a pitch, because then, seeing a pitch in the hitting zone, he'll be surprised by it. Aggressiveness is his operative approach.

On the other hand, his "control" is based on using his eyes when he gets to the plate. That's how he steers the bat to the ball. He hits the brakes only when he sees a pitch he does *not* want to swing at. His eyes are essential for that discipline. That control.

Corey Myers received a $2 million signing bonus from the Arizona Diamondbacks. He struggled early in his professional career at Class A South Bend in the Midwest League. As his confidence waned, his aggressiveness at bat left him. His approach went from thinking no one could get him out to, "Well, I just hope to hit the ball." He began to think too much in the box. And see too little. It's very difficult to be aggressive when you don't recognize the object of your aggression. It's hard to be *ready* to swing when you're a "hoper." It's harder to "pull the trigger."

In contrast, many hitters say, "I'm goin' up there hackin'." They're the hitters who invariably will be out of control. Undisciplined. [See *After-words*, "DISCIPLINE"] Their focus is on swinging — without seeing. Their foot is on the accelerator — and they don't see the wall they're about to crash into. Yes, sometimes they manage to avoid the wall — the ball hits the swinging bat. No credit to them. Flailing is not hitting. Hacking is not a philosophy.

In 1989, Jack Clark was struggling badly, hitting below .200 just before the All-Star break. He had five or six home runs and not very many RBI. I was asked to visit with him. First, I watched his at-bats for a few games. It wasn't difficult to recognize what he was doing to himself. He was "hackin'" at everything. The pitchers, seeing this, refused to throw him strikes. He kept "hackin'" and he kept striking out or making weak contact. Getting himself out.

When we got together, I wanted to get his attention immediately. I told him he should aspire to lead the league in walks during the second half of the season. I'm usually not so arbitrary with a hitter. He was not pleased; he told me he was paid "to hit the ball out of the yard."

At this point, let me offer the reader three names: Mark McGwire, Barry Bonds, Frank Thomas. These players have very frequently "hit the ball out of the yard" over the years. Yet, they are always at or near the top of the list of league-leaders in bases-on-balls. (And I do not include intentional walks.) They are discriminating hitters. They swing at hittable pitches! They are patient, rather than anxious, hitters. *That is why they are so successful.* They will take a walk. They are surely aggressive, and just as surely under control.

Jack Clark, after a more tactful explanation from me, did admit that he was not seeing the ball, because he was being too aggressive — out of desperation. He led the league in walks in the second half of 1989. Just as significantly (more so?), he raised his batting average to .242, had 94 RBI for the season — and went "out of the yard" 26 times. More control was his need, not the accelerated aggressiveness he'd been bringing to his at-bats. Every hitter must learn to strike the proper balance.

You recall that Carlos Delgado attributed his success to learning to see the ball better. He also became a more patient hitter. Add his name to the list with Canseco, Bonds, McGwire. His 2000 total, 123 walks, established a career high, by far. And add Oakland's Jason Giambi, the American League's MVP for the 2000 season, to that list (as many walks as RBI — 137).

Oakland has always valued the base-on-balls. Sandy Alderson, the general manager during my nine years with the A's, was greatly concerned with on-base percentage as one important indicator of a hitter's effectiveness. My appeal to a few reluctant players was that a walk helped their batting average. An undisciplined at-bat usually resulted in an out — and their average went down. A walk avoided that out, got them on base for the team — and kept the average from going down. This philosophy still prevails throughout the organization. Minor leaguers are taught to be patient — as well as aggressive.

As patient as Carlos Delgado may be, he remains an aggressive hitter, first and foremost. "My approach," he says, "is that every time I go up to hit, I'm ready. You never know when they're going to throw one down the middle, so you have to be aggressive." That's what he means by being "ready." Prepared to hit the good pitch, but also prepared to lay off the unacceptable one.

Delgado won the 2000 Hank Aaron Award as the top hitter in his league. (Todd Helton won it in the National League.)

Item: On August 7, 2000, two first-place teams played each other at Yankee Stadium. The Seattle Mariners defeated the Yankees, 11-1. A New York writer wrote the next day about the body language of Yankees pitcher Orlando Hernandez, after his pitches had been whacked by Seattle hitters. He conjectured that it looked as if Hernandez was standing on the mound, asking, "How did this happen?"

The writer, Jack Curry, provided the answer to the hypothetical question: "It happened because the Mariners were patient. They made a rusty Hernandez work deep into counts, and they treated a pitcher who was considered one of the best in the American League in April like an impostor."

Aggressiveness *and* patience provided the 11 runs. It is the balanced approach of all good hitters. And of successful teams.

Note: The eight major league teams in 2000 post-season play were the teams (four in each league, of course) to lead their leagues in — you guessed it, bases on balls.

Item: In his first year as a big-leaguer, Colorado first baseman Todd Helton was excessively aggressive. During one particular at-bat, he jumped to hit a pitch that was over his head. (The hit-and run play was *not* on.) Cubs pitcher Kevin Tapani remembers being able to fool Helton easily with changeups. "No more," says Tapani. "Now, you just have to hope he hits the ball at someone."

Helton, in 2000, became the eighth player in major league history to walk 100 times — and have 200 hits, 100 runs, and 100 RBI, all in the same season.

Many players, rookie leaguers and big leaguers, have acknowledged to me that they are anxious or excited hitters. Let's make a distinction here. The word "anxious" derives from "anxiety," meaning fear or worry. Many hitters fear striking out. They've admitted this to me. Their behavior reflects their fear.

Their goal is to put the ball into play as early in the count as possible. By doing so, they avoid the dreaded strikeout. The bad news is that they also avoid having a controlled, effective at-bat — seeing a good pitch to hit. The irony is that this behavior hardly qualifies as aggressive behavior, though it appears as such. The mentality is actually one of self-protection. It isn't control either; it is defensiveness. A giving in to frustration or fear. [See Chapters 9 and 10]

White Sox slugger Frank Thomas came back from a terribly frustrating and "embarrassing" 1999 season. By the season's end, his at-bats were often virtual giveaways. Thomas's head came off the ball, his swing produced pop-ups, and he pushed his bat in front of him, hoping (that word again) to make contact — protecting himself against the pitch. It was hardly the approach with which he had established himself as a premier slugger — and hitter. In the past, he had been aggressive and under control; in 1999 he became defensive and non-aggressive. The 2000 season showed him at his best once again, thanks to a re-established aggressive approach — now *truly* under control.

Item: From *The Sporting News*, September 9, 2000: "Lately pitchers have exploited...[Toronto third baseman Tony Batista] to send him into a deep slump. Pitchers are are sending the pitch to the plate a little too high, even for Batista [who loves the ball up] to reach, and offsetting it with out-of-the-zone breaking balls. The strategy, combined with the anxiety of an impatient pull hitter, put Batista's batting average at an even .100 over 50 at-bats in a 12-game span."

Item: In Philadelphia, on September 24, 2000, the New York Mets clinched the wild card spot in the National League's Eastern Division. First baseman Todd Zeile's fourth homer of the trip, after a very slow start in the month of September, sealed the deal for the Mets. Zeile's home run was to right-center field, a good sign for the hitter, who said he felt good again because of his patience, as indicated by the fact that the ball went "the other way." He had stayed in control of himself.

Said Zeile, "When you go through a cold stretch, you have a tendency to try to get out of it now, now, now. So I was hitting the first thing that came over the plate [or *anywhere near* it, as I had witnessed], putting bad swings on the ball and getting myself out. I've always been a guy that takes the count deep... I had to get back to that."

An excited, impatient hitter is out of control. Russian roulette may be exciting, but it can kill. An excited hitter is dangerous to himself. Alfredo Griffin was an excited player — in the batter's box and on the basepaths. One day in '85, Oakland was playing a doubleheader and Alfredo was leading off. I was witness to an incredible feat. Alfredo had eight at-bats in the two games and put the first pitch into play in all of those at-bats. He made eight outs.

The next day, I casually walked over to him on the field and put my arm around the shoulders of this fine, upbeat man. "Alfredo," I said in my most diplomatic manner, "Don't you think you might want to see more pitches, be more discriminating, more under control? *Especially* as a lead-off hitter."

He responded with his typical smile, "Don't worry, big guy. They've got me batting eighth tonight." He never hit leadoff for the A's again.

Premier Yankee shortstop Derek Jeter is proud to be an aggressive hitter. The Yankees are pleased he is an aggressive hitter. But the Yankees, like the Oakland A's, have established the reputation as a team of being patient and disciplined (controlled), as well, at the plate.

A former teammate, Tim Raines, spoke glowingly about Jeter to Buster Olney of *The New York Times*. "Before his career is over, he's going to be recognized as one of the best who ever played the game — I really believe that," Raines said of the shortstop.

But Raines remarked at length on the need for Jeter, as good as he is, to improve himself as a hitter by being more consistently under control during his at-bats. Though being aggressive serves a hitter well, Raines said that Jeter sometimes made up his mind to swing, "regardless of where [the pitch] is." If a pitch is out of the hitting area, or if a breaking ball moves out of the hitting zone, a hitter — Jeter included — cannot recognize either pitch, and puts a surprised swing on the ball.

It is an elementary lesson for hitters: if you program your mind to swing, you're *not* programming it to first *see*.

Jeter acknowledged the issue. "When you're going good… it's easy to lay off of it," he said. "It's not often during the season that you're zoned in. You tend to get yourself out. You say to yourself, 'OK, I'm going to jump on the first pitch,' and you end up swinging at a bad pitch."

It's an elementary lesson for hitters: you must program your eyes, as well as your muscles.

Raines pointed out, at this point, the difference between Jeter and Boston shortstop Nomar Garciaparra (who won his second consecutive American League batting title in 2000). "Garciaparra goes to the plate looking for a pitch in a certain area and he takes advantage of it. Jeter will make contact, but he won't do the type of damage he could."

Cleveland's manager, Charlie Manuel, the team's former hitting coach, identified the team's offensive problem early in the 2000 season. "They're [the hitters] not waiting for pitches they can drive." Easy to identify, as Jeter has noted. Harder to achieve.

The aggressive mentality brings a hitter to the plate expecting to swing at a pitch in the hitting zone. But the eyes must control that mentality, when the pitch is *not* in that zone. If the ball *is* in the zone — muscles, do your stuff.

Item: New York Mets pitcher Bobby Jones one-hit the San Francisco Giants in the 2000 National League Division Series. After the game, Giants second baseman Jeff Kent said, "We just tried to do too much against Jones. I call him a softie; he just puts the ball in there and makes you hit it. We were not controlling our aggressiveness…"

Said Mets catcher Mike Piazza of Jones's approach to the Giants hitters: "He was preying off [their] aggressiveness."

When hitters who are typically controlled hitters become excited because of circumstance or statistics, my advice is consistent. Go the other way — to the opposite field. An excited or anxious hitter usually jumps at the ball — leaves too early. Going the other way allows him to stay back longer. It also allows him to track the ball longer, the ball getting deeper before he commits. It encourages the relaxation process, as well, because the hitter knows he wants to wait, rather than go early — jump out at the ball. This is somewhat comparable to what was discussed in the previous chapter about an at-bat, during which the hitter knows he's only going to take pitches. His sight of the ball improves, because seeing the ball is his only task. But his additional responsibility is to make hard contact.

Chicago Cubs hitting coach Jeff Pentland called Cubs outfielder Brant Brown "an aggressive and emotional hitter." Pentland implored Brown to "settle down" — to wait for the ball to come to him, instead of being too aggressive in attacking it. Brown responded by driving the ball to all fields.

Atlanta Braves centerfielder, Andruw Jones, worked on behaviors that would countervail his past tendencies to be overly-aggressive at bat. His fine 2000 season illustrated his successful achievement of this behavioral goal. "I'm much more patient at the plate," Jones said, adding that he still considers himself to be an aggressive hitter. His numbers validated both points he made.

In May of that season, after having been a single shy of hitting for the cycle, Jones was asked about the near-miss of the cycle. Jones responded with talk about his approach, not the results. "I'm just being patient and relaxed," he reiterated. [See Chapter 11] I don't swing at *their* pitch; I swing at *my* pitch."

Finally, emphasis must be given to the point that a hitter's agenda is not only to hit, but to hit successfully. An aggressive mentality is essential for any effective competitor. Achievers are aggressive: "I'll *hit* the ball hard." But achievers are also smart and self-confident: "I'll see the ball well and [as Jones noted above] I'll get *my* pitch to hit." They have the aggressiveness to go after it as soon as they see it. They have the control to wait until they see what they want, as Raines emphasized earlier.

Needless to say, hitting with two strikes changes the idea of waiting for the perfect hitter's pitch. But it shouldn't change the idea of swinging aggressively. Patty-caking a ball into play may serve a specific game situation, but it isn't a mental approach that applies to all two-strike hitting. The hitter may not have the luxury of being as selective as he can be early in the count, but when he does go after a pitch, he should do so with aggressiveness, not caution, as a general rule. Seeing it well is caution enough.

But too much of a good thing becomes a bad thing. The Greeks said it 2,500 years ago: "Nothing in excess." During the 2000 season Seattle Mariners first baseman John Olerud acknowledged that he may have taken pitches for ball four that he could have hit. This, with men in scoring position. With his great hitter's eye, Olerud's instinct, he said, is to take pitches that are not in the strike zone. He said he was going to try to be more aggressive. He finished the season with 103 RBI, 102 walks.

Ted Williams did just fine with his discriminating eye — and an accompanying aggressive mentality. The situation will often dictate which side of the balance beam a hitter must move to.

16

REMEMBER

• A balanced mental approach means being aggressive while being under control.

• Aggressiveness is swinging; control is seeing the ball well, which allows you to swing at appropriate pitches.

• Attacking the ball without fear of striking out is essential to aggressive, effective hitting.

• Knowing the strike zone is essential to being a controlled hitter.

• When you sense you're losing control, hit the ball to the opposite field. You'll track the ball longer and deeper into the hitting zone; you'll stay back longer; it will help you relax your swing — the bat will get through the hitting zone quicker.

• Understand that a walk has value; that on-base percentage is one indicator of successful hitting; that a walk helps a batting average because, in addition to putting you on base, it keeps you off the bench — as an out! In addition, it benefits the team to have you on base, so it serves a greater purpose, as well.

• Remember that the best hitters hit *their* best pitch, not the pitcher's best pitch.

• Two-strike hitting should not be defensive hitting. It is just less selective hitting. Widen your strike zone and when you see what you want, let it fly.

• With two strikes, continue to look for the ball. Avoid guessing, particularly guessing breaking ball. (Many hitters worry about the breaking ball with two strikes on them, because they don't want to be surprised, have a bad swing, and be embarrassed.) Guessing like that with two strikes is an indication of self-doubt — and it's dangerous. It's Russian roulette with a bat. If anything, look for the fastball and adjust to the breaking ball. But look, rather than guess.

CHAPTER 3

Setting Your Goals vs. Living Others' Expectations

"The secret of success is constancy of purpose."
— Benjamin Disraeli

Every successful person I've ever met has been a goal setter. Setting goals gives an individual a sense of purpose and a sense of direction at the same time. A relentless will keeps him focused on that purpose. *His* purpose.

A baseball player must know how to distinguish between appropriate goals and inappropriate goals. Furthermore, he should know that what others expect of him has no place on his list of goals. Without that understanding his purpose is likely to be counterproductive; he's just as likely to head in the wrong direction.

⚾

Result goals are not within the hitter's control, therefore they are inappropriate. It's all well and good to have the desire to hit .320, to knock in an impressive number of runs and so on. But a hitter can't dictate what happens to the ball after he hits it. He *is* able to control his thoughts and actions before and during his swing. That's where his concern and focus should be.

Being well prepared and well conditioned, being relaxed, seeing the ball well, staying within himself, knowing how to make adjustments, being able to focus on the immediate task at hand — these are simply stated but formidable goals. They are all **behavior goals** — and those are the ones a hitter can work on daily. He cannot work on his batting average, which is an end. His behaviors are the means to that end, but even impeccable behavior doesn't guarantee the result of getting hits.

In 1985, Oakland's AA minor league team in Huntsville, Alabama, won the Southern League Championship. On the team's roster were Jose Canseco, who became the league's MVP that year, Louie Polonia, Stan Javier — and an infielder named Ray Thoma. During one particular three-game series, I saw Ray hit the ball as consistently hard as any player I've ever seen. Including big leaguers. But he had no luck, in terms of what he called "having something to show for it."

He meant hits. But what he had "to show for it" — if he were only capable of getting past his frustration, was a consistently effective approach to hitting.

At-bat after at-bat, he hit line drives and balls toward the gap. Every one was either at an infielder or run down by an outfielder. He'd come back to the dugout, the frustration mounting with each at-bat, and as he went by me, I'd say to him, "Way to swing the bat, Ray," or "Stay right there, Ray," or "Great at-bat, Ray; keep it going just like that." Of course, I was reinforcing his approach: his being on every ball with his eyes, his aggressive and controlled stroke, and in a relaxed state — which I was afraid he'd lose as the frustration intensified. The results: 11 consecutive outs.

On his 12th at-bat against this same team, he hit a screamer — a line drive right over the third-base bag. The third baseman dove to his right and picked the ball off the bag with a backhand stab. Ray was oh-fer-12 for the series. On the way past me in the dugout — before I had a chance to say anything — he put his hand up in front of my face and told me to "shut up." Everyone in the dugout, myself included, burst out laughing. Even Ray let a smile break out — eventually.

He was tired of hearing about how well he was hitting, because the results didn't reinforce his approach, and my words, though true, were "getting tired." He wanted hits, not philosophy — and that is what puts so many players into slumps. Without those hits, they start to press and their entire approach — mental and mechanical — breaks down. They lose the courage of their conviction. They lose their trust. They forget their **behavior goals** as they desperately grasp for results. (Remember the anecdote about Jack Clark in the preceding chapter?) You should not accept an attitude such as this to control you, if one of your long-term goals is to be a consistent and effective hitter.

A more recent occurrence took place while I was a member of the Florida Marlins staff. The major league team was playing a home game in Miami (1996?). In that particular game, Marlins outfielder Jeff Conine had two fine at-bats, with no hits to show for them. He'd seen the ball well, put good swings on the ball and hit it hard each time. Right at a fielder. The result: two outs. His third at-bat was identical to the previous two.

Conine returned to the dugout and sat down next to me, giving me a look that I interpreted as saying, "Well, wise guy, what do you have to offer?"

He held his look. I said, "You've got to work on your placement."

Jeff Conine is an intelligent person — with a keen sense of humor. He knew what my serious answer would have been, as Ray Thoma had known. Conine smiled.

During his next at-bat, Conine, a right-handed hitter, was fooled by a pitch he obviously wasn't looking for. (Guessing?!) He awkwardly flailed at a pitch down and away — well out of the hitting zone — and somehow made contact. The ball took flight like a wounded bird and landed just inside the right-field foul line and just beyond the groping reach of the first baseman. A hit.

He was left stranded on base. When he returned to the dugout at the end of the next half-inning, he again sat next to me. This time he had a bemused look on his face as he waited for me to speak again. "Much better," I said, with a straight face.

Jeff Conine understood the irony and understood the point I was really trying to make: good behavior doesn't always bring statistical results. Nor does bad behavior guarantee failure. Luck can influence our world, true enough. But a hitter who consistently approaches his at-bats effectively will be a greater influence on his performance. Those whose goals are related to their batting average will develop bad behavioral habits. His numbers, as Conine well knew, were beyond his control. [See Chapter 11]

The reason we can control a **goal of behavior** should be clear enough. We choose to behave one way or another. We choose to think one way or another. Choice is freedom, and though a hitter can't steer a ball through the infield or into the gap, or over the fence, he certainly is free to steer his thoughts and thereby control his behavior. The key word here is thoughts. If we buckle to our feelings — frustration, disappointment, and self-doubt, for example — we will allow those emotions to get in the way of our thinking process. We'll then act out what we're feeling, rather than what we should be thinking.

If a hitter understands this tendency — a very human one — he should put at the top of his list of goals the regular monitoring of his thoughts and actions. He should create the habit of knowing what he's thinking before he gets into the hitter's box and as he's getting ready to hit. Any thought beyond seeing the ball and being easy will distract him and complicate his approach. Having a simple approach should be a most valued goal. (Some **behavior goals** will be noted at the end of this chapter.)

A distinction should be made between goals and **expectations,** just so hitters recognize the difference between what they want for themselves and what others want from them. Many of the problems players meet are the result of the pressure and anxiety they feel because they consider themselves responsible for pleasing others. These "others" may be well-meaning people. Often, they are loving relatives or friends. But their needs should be irrelevant to the player. That, too, is easier said than done, but for the player it's an important understanding and a necessary behavior.

If, in fact, a player has this issue, the quicker he addresses the person(s) presenting these expectations, the better off he'll be. Honesty and directness are essential. Tact is advised. The truth doesn't have to take the form of a hammer, but it has to make impact enough to be felt.

Over the years, many players have told me they feel pressure from **expectations** beyond those people they can deal with personally. What a player reads or hears in the media or from management people and fans can provoke and intensify his feelings of responsibility. The only solution is to tune out and toughen up. It must be understood that the more talent a person has, the greater the expectations of others will be. The "burden" of talent that players talk to me about is a burden they've consented to have put on their backs. Don't consent. Focus on your understanding of how to hit, rather than on the intrusive needs of others.

Outfielder Jeromy Burnitz has established himself as a very respectable power hitter. As a very highly-touted rookie with the New York Mets in 1993, he was given no margin for error — no patience for experience. He was traded to Cleveland, where he fared no better. In 1997, Milwaukee "put him out there" and let him play himself into his potential.

Davey Lopes, who managed the player with the Milwaukee Brewers in 2000, had this to say about Burnitz: "Some players, for whatever reason, it takes a while for them to establish themselves. I don't know everything that has happened to Jeromy in the past, but you see that a lot in this game.

"When guys are high draft picks, there are a lot of expectations. They are expected to get to the big leagues quickly, and they are expected to perform. Some guys don't respond well under those circumstances. Personally, I always thought it was easier for guys to sneak in the back door, so to speak."

Great talent can't "sneak in the back door." However, it can — he can — walk through the door of *his* choice. The one that leads to his understanding of how to set appropriate goals for performance, rather than the one that leads to a room full of people who want to be gratified immediately by results.

To think that veteran players — hitters, in these cases — are not susceptible to such expectations is to not understand the human condition. Elite athletes want to succeed. Ken Griffey, Jr., is an elite athlete. He wanted very much to show his greatness in his hometown of Cincinnati, after having signed to play with the Reds before the 2000 season. The Reds fans and media expected no less from him.

He did not get off to a start that reflected his past performance and his ability. What it reflected was the pressure he felt to succeed. Pressure not diminished, one would guess, by the presence of his father, a coach in the Reds' dugout.

Even with his past success, the frustration was severe enough for Griffey, Jr., to say that he wanted to change his uniform number to the one he wore in Seattle — # 24. (He was wearing # 30, which his father had worn as a Cincinnati player.) He knew very well that the # 24 he was requesting has already been retired to honor Tony Perez, who would be inducted into the Baseball Hall of Fame in mid-summer. The request was refused by the Reds' organization. Griffey, Jr., "recovered." [See Chapter 8]

A most dramatic example of buckling to the expectations of others came during the 2000 Olympic games in Sydney, Australia. French two-time Olympic champion Marie-Jose Perec, who was to run against Australia's Cathy Freeman, retreated from the games, leaving Sydney abruptly. The pressure of her country's expectations had gotten to her. "I'm so frightened," she said publicly, and disappeared shortly thereafter.

Finally — and I must state this in the negative for emphasis on the behavior itself — don't ever be an apologist for your performance. People will ask, "What happened?" or "How come you're not hitting?" or other questions about "what's wrong" when you're struggling. Every time you apologize, you diminish yourself, make yourself more vulnerable, and weaken your mental make-up.

How then to respond to such questions? I advise players to just say, "I'm working on it." You do not owe anyone an apology, and you should only explain your circumstance to those who truly understand what the game — and hitting — and *you* are all about. Explain, don't apologize — if you care to explain at all.

Trust in your talent, and rely on your behavior goals to get you out of whatever struggles you encounter. And remember that if you're hitting the ball hard consistently, you're *not* struggling! You've got the eyes; the ball doesn't.

 REMEMBER

• Set **behavior goals**, which you can control, rather than **result goals**, which you cannot.

• Monitor your thoughts regularly, recognizing when your feelings are getting in the way of your thinking — and interfering with your appropriate hitting approach.

• Be certain to establish **functional goals**, so as not to be made dysfunctional by results or other people's expectations.

• Establish individual goals that can be worked on daily as a hitter. They may include practice and game goals, such as:

-Disciplined batting practice
-Seeing the ball well in BP
-Having a purpose in every BP round
-Reminding yourself of mechanical cues in on-deck circle
-Stepping out of box at coaching self during an at-bat
-Being mentally ready on every pitch
-Establishing your strike zone through discipline
-Being an aggressive hitter, under control
-(Add your own)

CHAPTER 4

Self-Coaching:

Making Adjustments in the Heat of the Battle

"If you can keep your head when all about you are losing theirs...you'll be a Man, my son!"
— Rudyard Kipling, *If*

Infantrymen in the midst of battle can't ask their drill sergeant what he thinks is best to do. Sailors on the firing line cannot refer to their *Blue Jackets Manual*. Whatever is required at that moment, in that circumstance, is their exclusive responsibility.

Self-coaching is simply (?) the technique of reminding yourself how to respond to the circumstance — to the moment — during the heat of battle. Hitters, though their plight is not life-threatening, face the "heat" on a regular basis. (Actually, I've come across some hitters who thought their lives *were* "on the line" when they played baseball. Their perspective was, of course, distorted.) [See Chapter 7]

My message to professional players — and it also applies to amateur baseball players who hope to play at higher levels of competition — is that each of them is the most important coach he'll ever have. By this I do not mean to imply that a player won't gain abundant and valuable insights from others. But only the player himself can integrate this information into behavior. Or *not* be able to apply what he's learned.

This is the responsibility of a hitter as self-coach: to help himself understand, use, and appropriately adjust what he learns —

26

from others or from game experience. He must know what works for him and what does not work. He may hear recommendations from others, but he must learn — in the long run — to trust himself. Such learning is a process. The less experienced the hitter, the longer the process.

Conventional wisdom tells us that baseball is a game of adjustments. The player ultimately makes adjustments. Some are necessary; some are not necessary; some do more harm than good. It's a hitter's responsibility to know which to make, when to make them, and how to make them. It all starts with self-study, which is a major part of the curriculum in the school of wisdom.

Seattle pitcher Jamie Moyer, not known for imposing "stuff," nevertheless has been a very effective pitcher over the years. He studies opposing hitters. Scrutinizes them. He has put together a notebook with information on just about every hitter he has faced. He certainly knows more about some of them than they know about themselves.

The "study" includes hitters' patterns, strengths, and weaknesses. Moyer's greatest discovery is not about these tendencies, however. The greatest revelation to him is that many hitters never adjust. They will continue to behave in the same way, despite apparent inability to get the job done. And Moyer will continue to take advantage of such hitters.

The point here is that the pitcher is only doing to the hitter what the hitter allows him to do. That is not acceptable behavior for any hitter who aspires to excellence.

It is unacceptable for a hitter to struggle for two weeks without considering that his mental approach may be the cause of his struggles. It's certainly better for him to make a necessary adjustment after a bad game. Better still after a bad at-bat. *After a pitch* is the ideal!

In order to do this, the hitter has to coach himself throughout the course of an at-bat. He does *not* have to be obsessive about it.

("If it ain't broke, don't fix it.") But when his approach breaks down, he should know why and put a thoughtful strategy into play as quickly as possible.

Here are a few "essentials" to remember:

1) A HITTER MUST EXAMINE QUICKLY "WHAT'S HAPPENING" DURING HIS AT-BATS.

Thinking takes place out of the batter's box, not in it. (See the ball; be easy is the focus in the box.) The problem may be **psychological** (e.g., having distracting thoughts or trying to do too much); **philosophical** (e.g., missing a pitch because he tried to pull a ball that was an outside pitch); **mechanical** (e.g., forgetting, before stepping into the box, his key for establishing lower body balance).

No one knows what you're thinking but you. No one can coach you in the middle of an at-bat but you.

2) A HITTER MUST HAVE THE PRESENCE OF MIND TO STEP OUT OF THE BOX AND TAKE CONTROL OF HIS THOUGHTS.

While on the Florida Marlins' coaching staff a few years ago, I watched one of our better hitters have the particular problem of taking fastballs "right there" for called strike three. After seeing this happen too many times, I confronted him when he sat down next to me in the dugout, after having done it again. "You're guessing up there, aren't you?" I asked.

He told me he'd gotten into the habit of guessing with two strikes after having been embarrassed by a few of his wild-swing-third strikes on breaking balls out of the hitting zone. Unfortunately, he went from one embarrassment to another, and now he guessed breaking ball and felt foolish when called out on a fastball right down the middle of the plate. At this point, he was relieved to discuss the problem.

From then on, whenever he had two strikes on him, he called time, stepped out of the box, and coached himself. He simply told himself to track the ball. He didn't *guess* fastball, but *anticipated* it and adjusted to the breaking ball. This he could do because sighting the ball was on his mind, rather than thinking about what kind of pitch was coming. At both extremes of behavior in the recent past, he'd forgotten that essential key.

The strategy was easy enough, but its application was only possible after his *awareness*. Because of that first step, he was able to know what to do and coach himself *during his at-bat*, becoming more consistently effective.

3) A HITTER MUST COACH HIMSELF IN POSITIVE TERMS, TELLING HIMSELF WHAT HE WANTS TO DO, RATHER THAN WHAT NOT TO DO.

Michael Davis, an outfielder with the Oakland A's in the mid-'80s, was the first of many big league hitters to indicate to me that he was using negative commands to coach himself during at-bats. For example, Michael would tell himself to "lay off the high fastball." When the high fastball came, he swung. The mind computes image words. It doesn't hear "don't"; it hears "high fastball." The eyes see the high fastball; the mind says, "There it is, go get it." The negative instruction worked at cross purposes with the hitter's intent. Telling himself what he doesn't want to do is ineffective self-coaching on the hitter's part.

The hitter, in this case, Michael, simply changed his self-coaching tactic. He would say, "Look for the ball..." (In whatever location he *wanted*).

Andruw Jones benefited greatly when Merv Rettenmund signed on with Atlanta Braves before the 2000 season. Rettenmund has the deserved reputation of being a premier hitting coach in the big leagues. Part of his great success has been his self-effacing style, which allows the hitter to take more responsibility for himself.

Jones was asked about his success under Coach Rettenmund's watchful eye. His response: "My coach is myself. 'You're the one who has to go out and do it.' That's what he tells me all the time."

I have seen hitters come back and ask the hitting coach, "What did you see?" after every at-bat. I've witnessed hitters asking just about *everyone* in the dugout that question. Rettenmund's typical response: "What did you *feel?*" And I would ask, "What were you *thinking?*"

We can't solve problems unless we're aware of them. A hitter's awareness is crucial. He must learn what he is thinking and what he is physically (mechanically) feeling before he can formulate a strategy for making an adjustment. That's self-coaching.

It's not a matter of not understanding what to do during competition. It is a matter of letting other thoughts pre-empt that understanding. As I have often said and written, the two words I hear most from athletes are, "I know." But though those words may excite me in a classroom, they aren't enough in athletic competition.

Australia's Olympic superstar, Cathy Freeman, before the 400-meter race in the 2000 Olympic Games, on what she has called one of the biggest nights of her life, remembered to coach herself effectively. She repeated, over and over, "Do what you know. Do what you know..." That coaching reassured her; it relaxed her — it reminded her.

 **REMEMBER**

• Take the responsibility of learning how to coach yourself during your at-bats.

• When you're unhappy about what's going on during an at-bat, step out of the box and make yourself aware of the problem.

• Out of the box, remember your individual mental or mechanical key, as it applies to your awareness.

• Coach yourself by telling yourself what you want to-do, rather than what you don't want to do, before stepping back in the box.

• Talk from your brain, rather than your emotions of the moment.

• Exhale deeply, to relieve possible tension.

• In the box, look for the ball, and be easy.

CHAPTER 5

Self-Talk

(Talk Right; Walk Right)

"Our everyday language can be viewed as a brain tool."
— J. Samuel Bois, *Explorations in Awareness*

Language is the tool we use to do most of our thinking. The better the tool, the more effective we can be in doing the job. Thinking is talking to ourselves. The better our brain operates, using effective language, the better our muscles will respond.

"The body is a fool," I tell players. "It will do whatever it's told." If the muscles learn the right habits, they'll keep repeating the behavior over and over again. The problem is they are often taught the wrong lessons — not because of the teacher's intention, but because of the teacher's language.

The previous chapter focused on the importance of a hitter learning to coach himself. A reference was made to the hitter's need to tell himself what he wants to do, rather than what he doesn't want to do. This of course, is the stating of functional, task-oriented talk expressed in positive language. It is essential to good coaching and teaching; it becomes essential to learning the proper mental approach to hitting.

Much of what infants learn is the result of negative teaching. A couple of examples: "No, you mustn't touch that glass," and "Don't go near the hot stove." This is understandable, because parents react to something the infant is about to do — or already has done — that can be harmful to himself or to a valued object. Negative lessons are frequently used by parents from their child's

32

birth until he is six or seven years old. This, says Jacques Barzun, is because a child is a "simian" — a small animal who needs the "negative education" of having his environment controlled for him.

Very often (most often?), this approach lasts well beyond seven years. Research has indicated that by the time youngsters reach the teen years, they've heard "No" or "Don't" 40,000 times. That's powerful teaching, and the brain has learned the message well.

Too well, in the case of hitters. The self-talk hitters use — silently or out loud — is often a result of this training. The less they've heard positive language from parents, teachers, and coaches over the years, the less likely they are to able to coach themselves well — or, for that matter, to have a positive outlook about themselves.

◖◗

As a case in point, let me refer to an old favorite book of mine, one I bought as a teenager, written by a hitter I saw play many times in the old Polo Grounds in New York, where he was the first baseman for the New York Giants. The player was Johnny Mize; his book is called *How to Hit.* I still have the book. I first read it in 1953. And as I thought about writing the chapter on self-talk for *this* book, *that* book flashed into my mind.

What I remembered vividly related to the instructional keys. And here is the truth of the matter: I did not recall the keys. I did remember the urgent commands. "Don't forget ..."

I opened the book and found them. Twenty (!) "Don't forget's." *That* is what I remember. (As the reader has already seen, these chapters end with what to remember to do, rather than what *not* to do.)

◖◗

With that in mind, recall that the Pittsburgh Penguins had never beaten the Philadelphia Flyers in NHL Eastern Conference playoff competition. (At one time they went 15 years without winning in Philadelphia.) Game 2 of the 2000 playoffs was to be played in Philly.

Penguins goalie Ron Tugnett knew the power of negative talk. Yet, he said — with conviction, "We told ourselves, 'Let's not give ourselves negative thoughts by thinking we can't win here. If we won here, we wouldn't have to hear anymore we can't win here.'"

If you re-read that statement you'll find five negative words, and the word "have" — something imposed on the players by others. Not exactly an uplifting message. The right idea; the wrong delivery.

Even well-intentioned athletes succumb to negative language, despite their understanding of its power to hurt performance.

And this: In June of the 2000 season, struggling Houston Astros first baseman and pre-eminent hitter Jeff Bagwell, who was struggling but nevertheless got his 1,000th career RBI, said after the game, "I'm one of those 'The cup is half-empty' kind of guys. I'm so messed up. If I got 3,000 hits, I'd probably be thinking more about the 7,000 outs I've made." He has succeeded in spite of himself, one might say. Obviously, he has done — and said — something right.

I've dealt with hitters who tell themselves what to do in positive terms, but unfortunately they seek results they can't control, rather than behavior they can.

For example, at the beginning of September of the 2000 season, Florida Marlins second baseman Luis Castillo was embarrassed by his total of 10 RBI. He was hitting .224 with runners in scoring position and .395 with the bases empty. Why? Inappropriate self-talk.

"When I'm swinging [with men on base], I'm swinging at two bad pitches because I'm saying, 'I want a hit,'" Castillo explained. Focus on the result and you'll lose focus on the ball — and swing indiscriminately.

Earlier in the season, Castillo's teammate, outfielder Mark Kotsay, was also concerned with driving in runs — particularly with two out and men in scoring position. I asked him what he was saying to himself when he was in those situations. Answer: "I'm responsible [as a number-three hitter] for getting those runs in."

"How do you do that?" I asked. He answered that question as easily. "Just see the ball and drive it," he said.

"Just the way you approach every at-bat," I reminded. End of issue.

I've heard players at every level scold, criticize, and condemn themselves for making a mistake. Then they tell me they have little self-confidence. It should come as no surprise; negative self-talk does nothing to build confidence and everything to destroy it. We all make mistakes. The only way to get better is to tell ourselves what we want to do next time, rather than dwelling on what went wrong moments ago. *Or days ago*, since negative self-talk seems to intensify our memory of mistakes — and create a fear of repeating them.

And therein lies the big problem. The more a hitter focuses on what is wrong about him, what is wrong about his swing and what is likely to go wrong in his at-bats — the more likely it *will* go wrong. That's called a self-fulfilling prophecy: anticipate behaving in a certain way and you tend to behave right into the anticipation.

The answer should be obvious: *anticipate positive behavior!* Focus on function, not feelings. Talk to yourself about what you want to do as a hitter, rather than what you think you can't or shouldn't do. Catch yourself when you are trash-talking yourself. (**Awareness**, again, as a requirement for change!!) Then change your language; change the way you talk to yourself.

When I hear a player speaking negatively to himself or about himself, I ask him to describe a coach or manager who might come up to the player and speak to him that way. The descriptions I get are unprintable here. "So," I say to the player who has said the unprintable, "You are describing yourself."

As bad as it might feel at the moment, someone else's

negative talk to you, about you and about what you have or haven't done, is *easier to dismiss than your own negative talk to and about yourself.* Saying to yourself, "You stink," or calling yourself "an idiot" or "dummy" or "loser" or "gutless" is — to be polite — counterproductive.

In contrast, by using positive self-talk, you can train yourself to effectively recover from unhappiness and emotional self-assessment, thereby enhancing yourself and your performance, rather than diminishing both.

This is a process. Time and persistence are required. We don't unlearn bad habits overnight. The application of self-discipline and consistency to this issue can help train you to overcome other difficulties (such as giving in to tough times).

One prominent major league player reviewed with me the years we'd been working on his development of appropriate self-talk. He recalled how, in the beginning, the hardest thing was for him was to catch himself saying the negatives and then quickly convert them to positives. He didn't always believe what he was saying, he confessed, but he knew it was the right thing to say. But as time went by, it became easier to recognize and easier to correct. At the point of our discussion, this player (a future Hall-of-Famer, I am certain) said it was "scary" how natural it all had become for him.

Once he had begun, he worked hard at it. Had he started employing appropriate self-talk earlier, it would have been much easier. The younger you are, the less firm your bad habits have become. But a commitment must be made, and this player and others like him certainly made it.

Effective self-talk requires more than positive **language**. Also important are **timing** and **tonality**.

Timing: A hitter who hears himself speaking in negative terms should correct himself immediately, especially when the self-talk is expressed during competition. The longer negative thoughts control the muscles, the more difficult to change the muscles — and the thoughts.

Tonality: A hitter will send a mixed message to his muscles if he uses positive language and a harsh, negative tone. Even positive language, when presented with a tone of urgency will tense up the muscles and distract the focus. And saying, "That was just great," in a sarcastic tone doesn't qualify as being positive — or functional, if it *wasn't* great. I once heard a third-base coach scream in anger to a hitter in the batter's box, "Relax, dammit!" Not conducive to relaxation and not a positive message, after all. It is a tension-inducing delivery that is counterproductive. A calm, reassuring tone has a chance to get the message across. Not the tonality used with an infant, but not the tonality used on an ogre either. The hitter should find his own natural tone of voice, and say the right words in that voice.

Many people who desire to **think positively** have the false notion they can "block out" what they do not wish to think about by employing a negative command. As has been noted in a previous issue, a negative command brings attention to the image of what one doesn't want to think about. The example used referred to a hitter who told himself, "Don't swing at a high pitch." His attempt to "block out" that image only reinforced it. The brain computed "high pitch." That's the image word. He swung at the high pitch.

Let's say a person doesn't want to think of a white horse. He would, in this example, tend to say, "Don't think of a white horse." You know what he's thinking about, right? What should be understood is that the person can achieve what he wants by **changing his thought.** So he says, "Think of a brown cow." New thought; new image. The white horse has been *replaced.*

"See the ball." This is the most functional and appropriate replacement thought a hitter will ever have in the batter's box. Remember it; use it; value it.

Someone once said that we are what we think. When I'm at the end of a telephone conversation with a player, my sign-off line is always, "Be good to yourself." I am simply reminding the player to speak positively about himself and what he wants to do — and he will have a better chance to get it done well. This, of course, implies that if a player uses positive self-talk, he will come to *think* what he says — and *be* what he thinks. To talk right and thereby "walk right."

 **REMEMBER**

• Negative self-talk is usually a result of early teachings, warnings or experience. As an older individual, you are now capable of recognizing and controlling your self-talk. Give yourself positive instruction — as a hitter and as a person.

• Your muscles will do what they are told. Tell them the *right* things to do, in the right way — using positive language always.

• Make yourself aware of whatever negative messages you give yourself, so you can change them *immediately*.

• Employ an appropriate, calm tone of voice, rather than sarcasm or the tonality of anger or defeatism.

• When you wish to change your thought, *replace it* with one that serves and directs you in a positive way, rather than trying to block the undesirable thought out. Trying to block out a thought keeps your focus on the very thing you're trying to get rid of.

• Be good to yourself!

CHAPTER 6

Paying Proper Attention:
The Ability to Concentrate on Task

"A straight path never leads anywhere except to the objective."

— Andre Gide, *Journals*

The stronger and more sustained a hitter's ability to concentrate, the better he'll consistently see the ball well, which is his first objective. In the mental "book" of hitting, knowing what to focus on is the start, but knowing how to keep that focus is the finish.

As a young boy, I remember reading a number of books by the French aviator/writer, Antoine Saint-Exupery. One, in particular, seemed to speak to me specifically. (I was 12 years old; the book was *Flight to Arras*. I have it still.) In it was the following: "The field of consciousness is tiny. It accepts only one problem at a time. Get into a fist fight, put your mind on the strategy of the fight, and you'll not feel the other fellow's punches."

Concentration is pre-potent. It is first and most powerful as a performer's skill. That means any other circumstance, problem, or possible distraction becomes irrelevant to a hitter during his at-bat. His concentration leaves no room in his mind for any intrusive thought.

That's an ideal, an ideal truth — and attainable. So the development of concentration skills should be at the top of the list of goals for every hitter. And it requires regular attention. The most skillful hitter can still improve. Judging by my experience, even

40

big league hitters have plenty of room for improvement in this area. Most take their concentration for granted — until they begin to struggle, when their focus becomes broad and undisciplined.

A struggling hitter will think of all matters except the ball while he's batting. That's a loss of focus, due to a weakened mental discipline. Anyone who has ever sat through a boring lecture or read a dull book understands this perfectly. If it's important to listen to the lecture, you must discipline yourself to concentrate. If it's important to read and understand the book, you must discipline your eyes and mind to be attentive to the material. It can be a daunting task. But those who persist in attending to task can develop an intensity of concentration that has "a hunger to it."

During Instructional League programs with the organizations I've worked for, I'd perform a little demonstration to help the young players understand the differences in the intensity of their focus. The practice sessions were held in the morning — near mid-day — and when the sun was high in the sky, we gathered in a group.

I placed a newspaper page on the ground and held a magnifying glass knee high, over the paper. A broad, fuzzy circle appeared on the page. "This circle represents broad, poorly defined, casual or careless focus," I would say to the players.

I lowered the magnifying glass, moving it closer to the newspaper page. The circle became smaller and more defined, like a narrower and sharper focus. I then moved the magnifying glass lower — very close to the newspaper page. The circle became quite small and distinct — extremely narrow focus. The heat from the sun on that small area set the page on fire. *"That's* intensity," I said, though my words were not necessary; the players understood.

The working definition of concentration, as it applies to a hitter, is the ability to have an intense focus on the ball, to the exclusion of all else. The concentration, as noted earlier, will be

41

pre-potent. Mental discipline is required. Hitters should be aware of their thinking patterns and be disciplined enough to change broad, irrelevant thoughts to narrow, relevant cues. ("See the ball.")

It's very common for hitters to have several thoughts before and during their preparation for an at-bat. But when they get in the box, they must limit their thoughts and change their focus to a narrow, external one — the ball. This is a habit to cultivate. It should be an important **behavior goal**.

The better a hitter is doing, the more naturally his concentration skills are able to serve him. A hitter who is "going good" will say to me, "I'm not thinking about anything. I'm not thinking about concentrating." And that's why he's going good. His good behavior is more often than not rewarded by desired results. But when hitters begin to get poor results, they tend to change their approach. Their head fills with distracting thoughts. Their attention becomes divided. Their thinking becomes too broad, very often thinking about results — consequences. The future, rather than the moment.

One of the devices I use with players helps illustrate that effective concentration is pre-potent. When talking with a player in my home or hotel room, I show him a clock with a large second hand on it. Then I point out the minute hand. "This minute hand," I might say, "is on the one. It's five minutes after the hour." I then turn the face of the clock away from the player.

"Now, we're going to talk," I continue. "We're going to take care of the moment, one tick of that second hand at a time. We're going to focus on our thoughts and words — and, after a time, I'm going to turn the clock around so you can see it again."

Twenty minutes later or so, I stop the conversation and turn the clock. The minute hand is on the five: 25 after the hour. "Were you thinking about when the hand would be on the five?" I ask. "Were you conscious of the time passing?"

The player's answer is always, "No." *Always!* We were taking care of business, focusing on the task of the moment, rather than anticipating a future outcome. I remember my mother saying, when I was a boy many years ago, waiting impatiently for her to make a cup of hot chocolate for me, "A watched pot doesn't boil." It certainly didn't *seem* to.

Let's consider a common issue I've dealt with while working for major league organizations. It has to do with the personal matters players have to deal with away from the field. Sickness and/or death in the family, for example.

Players have come to me while caught in the dilemma of whether to stay with the team or leave to be with a family member, whatever the specific case may be. My question is always the same: "Can you do anything to help the situation at home by being there?" Moral support, practical support, the needs, and desires of the loved one are all considered.

If — *if* the answer is that there is no required reason to leave the team, then there is *nothing the player can do* to help the family situation. If he therefore chooses to stay with the team and play, he should focus on what he is doing, rather than what he's *not* doing. He should not allow himself to be distracted by guilt, since he's gone through a rational process and, presumably, spoken with family members at home about the decision.

So — play the game right.

Yankees third baseman Scott Brosius went through such a situation at the end of the 1999 season, when his father was dying. Brosius acknowledged that it was a tug-of-war between his mind and heart. His father wanted Scott to continue to play. And the player knew he would call regularly, doing whatever could be done under the circumstance. As difficult as it was, he was able to focus on task without distraction at the field. (He hit .375 in the World Series.)

Again, whatever possible cause for distraction may exist, a developed ability to concentrate on executing task will be stronger.

Item: Bill Russell, known as a single-minded competitor when he played for the Boston Celtics, was recently interviewed by a writer for *The New York Times*. The writer asked about a player being subjected to boos and taunting by crowds. Russell, named as the greatest player in the history of the NBA in 1980 by

Professional Basketball Writers Association, had this to say: "You know…my youngest child asked me one time, 'How do you handle people booing you and saying unkind things about you?'

"I said, 'Me personally, I never accepted the cheers, so I didn't have to worry about the boos.' When I was playing, there was nothing outside the lines."

"Nothing outside the lines." That's taking care of business. That's appropriate focus.

When a child is behaving well, a parent doesn't have to discipline that child. The discipline must be applied when the behavior is unacceptable. The same is true with a hitter. His "parent" — his rational mind — must step in and assert itself, disciplining the hitter, so as to stop him from operating out of his feelings (frustration, self-doubt, etc.) and get him back to — seeing the ball! How a hitter responds to adversity — whether it's the boos of a crowd or the burden of his responsibility [*See After-words*] will say a lot about his concentration skills specifically — and his character, in general.

The more disciplined a hitter is, meaning the more able he is to focus on task exclusively, the more successful he'll be over time. This doesn't always come "naturally." A persistent effort must be made. A concentrated effort, so to speak.

Shortstop Alex Rodriguez is mature beyond his years, as a hitter and as a person. He keeps things simple philosophically. "I'm a player who focuses on the now," he says. "That's what has made me successful. I focus on the present tense and not worry about the future or the past." Short and sweet.

Colorado first baseman Todd Helton has done fine for himself as well. His major asset as a hitter, he feels, is the great intensity, referred to previously. He brings it to every at-bat. *Intense* concentration, not *tense* muscles. Aggressiveness under control.

As a hitter, you must understand a few basic things if you're going to improve your concentration skills. First, understand what is possible to control and what is not. It's possible to control your thoughts, feelings, and behavior. You can't control external events, other people's thoughts and deeds, and consequences beyond your behavior.

- You can tell yourself what to do in positive terms.
- You can focus on the immediate, rather than past or future. (The next pitch — "the now" — is all that can be acted upon in the batter's box.)
- You can focus on your approach, instead of results — past or future.
- You can focus on the ball.

These simple understandings should be reiterated regularly, so they become a working philosophy for concentration. Players practice physical skills on a daily basis, but they usually just expect mental skills to develop themselves. They don't. Practice effectively to perform effectively — physically and mentally.

If you are going to defeat an enemy, you must be able to see him. If you are going to change bad habits or thoughts, you must be able to identify them. Three typical intrusions distract players from concentrating on the task they are about to perform. The source of these distractions relate to typical human needs and create a range of reaction from typical to dramatic. An elite athlete must remember that he doesn't allow ordinary behavior to be his goal. That he doesn't forfeit self-control to extreme responses. The distractions noted below cause a player to focus on himself, rather than the task he is about to execute.

1) INSTANT GRATIFICATION
The player, a precocious athlete since childhood, has had his way as a youth. As a hitter, he has succeeded against all

opposition. As he continues to play — becoming a professional — the "playing field levels." That is, the pitchers he faces are also talented. Lesser talents have fallen through the sieve. He's not used to struggling. He is used to immediate success. He hasn't ever suffered on a baseball field. He has always been instantly gratified. He knows nothing about making adjustments. His perspective is distorted, and he is frustrated. [See Chapter 7]

2) URGENCY

A player — hitter — perceives the importance of situational success. A pivotal at-bat in a big situation or game or series. ("I've gotta get the job done," or "I've gotta get this run in.") The sense of urgency creates tension, to begin with — and ends with the hitter thinking of consequences, thereby having divided attention. He doesn't see the ball well, has tight muscles [See Chapter 10], and is not likely to produce the result he seeks.

3) SELF-CONSCIOUSNESS

Many people are "pleasers." They want others to like them, acknowledge them as good players and people. They go out of their way to satisfy others, often at their own expense. A hitter who sees himself as such a person very often has a feeling of being watched, judged — evaluated — as he performs. He tends to have a limited self-trust, and he therefore seeks validation from others. Focus on task becomes a great effort, an unsuccessful one at times.

[Review Chapters 4 and 5 to address the above tendencies.]

In fact, it's often easier to practice mental skills than physical. You often do not need a baseball field. You can work on some concentration skills away from the field, sometimes just by sitting in a chair at home.

A few suggestions and practice activities will help you to develop your ability to concentrate effectively and consistently. You might vary or improve them as you become a more skilled practitioner.

But first consider this: "Mental toughness" is the term [See *After-words*] used as an ultimate compliment to an athlete. The degree to which you are able to fully and intensely concentrate on your task will indicate the degree of "mental toughness" you have. If it's worth having, it's worth the effort it takes to develop it. The persistent effort is part of the toughness. It will enhance your ability to concentrate on the task during the toughest of times.

MENTAL TOUGHNESS → THE ABILITY TO CONCENTRATE

REMEMBER — AND USE

CONCENTRATION EXERCISES

• <u>Be an observer.</u> Notice everything, especially details. This will bring you to be attentive to things you've never paid attention to before. It is a constant exercise in disciplining your mind and your eyes.

• Look at pictures hanging on the wall (or advertisement billboards at the ballpark). <u>Start by taking in the entire image, then keep narrowing your focus until you're centered on a very particular part of the picture/ad.</u> SEE it completely, noticing every detail. Stay on it with your eyes until you have committed the details to memory.

• Play the old kid's game (abbreviated version) of Concentration, using just a few cards from a deck of playing cards. Include one card for each number from 2 to 10. Have someone place the nine cards face down in random order. Then turn them up and view them quickly. Turn them face down again. Distract yourself for one minute. Then attempt to turn the cards over in order, starting with the deuce. As you become better able to do this — and decrease the time required to do it — add numbers from different suits, so you then have to turn two number-two's over, and so on. Be patient with yourself. You'll get better if your discipline is stronger than your frustration. (And that should be one of your goals on the field, as well!)

• A favorite of a number of big league players is the number grid. Make up a grid of 100 squares on a sheet of paper. (Make a bunch of photocopies.) Have someone else randomly fill in the blanks of a grid with numbers 01 to 99. Take the grid and go through it, crossing out the numbers in consecutive order. When you become stuck — seemingly unable to "find" the next number, stay with it. Stay with it, rather than quit. Work through to completion. Repeat this exercise as many time as you wish, having someone fill in the numbers in different spaces, of course. You will see improvement.

• Using the same exercise, time yourself. Keep a record of your times. Don't expect a continuous improvement. You'll have good days, and not-so-good days, just as you will on the field. The key is to be persistent, rather than giving in to a bad attempt. Stay the course. Focus on your task, not on your difficulty. A terrific exercise, because it serves many purposes.

• Using the same exercise, put on a talk radio program while you're working on the grid. Raise the volume as you become more skillful. This provides still another possible intrusion and distraction.

• Invent your own exercises, if you wish. But be diligent in whichever you are working on.

CHAPTER 7

Perspective:
Recognizing the Real

"It is the eye that makes the horizon."
— Ralph Waldo Emerson, *Circles*

Years ago, I stood in the outfield during batting practice with a minor leaguer who was playing on a Class A team in the Midwest League. His manager, coaches, and teammates had been waiting for me to arrive in Kane County, Illinois, so I could talk with this young man — and address what they all felt to be "his problem."

In talking with him, it became clear that what others considered to be a problem, he considered to be his exceptional desire to play in the big leagues. "I want it more than the other players do," he told me with pride. And perhaps he did.

During our conversation I asked him if he had a particular girl he was interested in and involved with. He did. I asked if he hoped to marry her, and he said they were actually close to becoming engaged. "You love her, then?" I asked. "Of course," he answered. "Really love her?" I persisted. "Of course!" he shouted, becoming annoyed with me.

"OK. What if I told you I had the power to absolutely guarantee that you'd make the big leagues, but the price you had to pay would be that I'd have to kill this girl. Or," I added, "you would have a wonderful life with the girl you love — nice children, and so on, but you'd never get to play in the major leagues. And you have to choose one or the other."

There was a prolonged silence, after which he said, "Harv, that's too hard a choice." He did have a problem.

The most obvious problem was one of perspective. He had an unhealthy one, to say the least. His vision was distorted. To his credit, he was willing to deal with it, and to my relief, he's now playing in the big leagues — and is happily married. That is good fortune, but he knows that every player aspiring to get to the big leagues doesn't get there. Nor would they kill to get there.

The big picture.

Perspective means point of view. The way a player/athlete sees his world off the field — the fuller view — will greatly influence the way he sees it on the field. And how he sees it will influence how he responds to it and addresses it. Optimistically or pessimistically. Accenting the positive or the negative. Anticipating performance as a challenge or as a threat. Being aggressive or being cautious — submissive. Or, perhaps, perceiving a big game as "do or I die" — because he believes the consequences in the small world (baseball) will lead to catastrophe in the big world "out there." You get the idea.

Control your mind to control your muscles.

The idea is that the athlete's perspective will dictate the body's behavior. Every time you're unhappy with any aspect of your performance, first and foremost examine your perspective. Examine whether you are performing out of your emotional system or your rational system. Are you acting out what you think — or what you feel? Your brain should be in control, telling you what to do (positive functional commands), rather than allowing your emotions to distract you by imposing how you feel onto your behavior. Your emotions may be based on concern with results and an anxiety related to negative anticipation. They may have been produced by what Shakespeare called "horrible imaginings."

A focus on self will produce an exaggerated and often distorted point of view. Surely, you've heard or read about many athletes who've said, "I have a completely different perspective now." The cause might have been a first child, a death in the family, or some other event that, first, puts the athlete's focus beyond himself or herself. Second, it allows the athlete to see a *reality* with life significance beyond *imaginings* related to the results of an athletic event. The athlete sees priorities that result in greater understanding, more relaxed muscles and more effective performance. The complexities of life allow us to better see the simplicity of the task we face. And it helps eliminate many of the "I gotta's" from our vocabulary.

Tennessee Titans defensive end Jevon Kearse came to his greater understanding the hard way. A father murdered before Jeron was born, a brother also murdered, another brother serving time in prison. His perspective? "Life goes on." He says it with a shoulder shrug that indicates sense not surrender. He has chosen to join life as it goes on, rather than stepping aside to let it go by or standing immobile in its path, letting it roll over him. A football game can't distort that perspective.

Neither should a baseball game.

To get it right, see it right.

Hold thoughts that are "big" — about yourself, your life or your sport — at a distance from you. A large object held too close to your face will block out the world beyond it. A large thought must be seen from a distance. That's why it's so easy to help a friend solve a problem, though the very same issue can confound you. "Step out of the frame, and it's easier to see the picture," I tell athletes.

A writer for *The New York Times* wrote that New Jersey Nets guard Stephon Marbury "resorted to looking at the big picture." Resorted?

Marbury himself explained how he coped with the difficulties his team was facing. "My mind is mentally worn down, but I won't break," he said, refusing to complain after a third consecutive routing of his team. "I know I'm able to get up every day and walk and talk. That's the best thing. There are people that are paraplegics that will never, ever walk. There are some people that would love to be in my situation…That's how I keep my mind in perspective."

Seeing the big picture does not mean giving in to the little picture. Playing with unacceptably low level of effort is giving in and using the big picture as an excuse. Playing hard every night and understanding what Marbury said is behaving like a mature athlete and an understanding adult at the same time.

The small picture.

During performance, a player's perspective must be narrowed so that, in the context of his specific activity, he must have a limited, small focus. Entirely different from the perspective of his life issues. Attention to the task at hand is all that should matter. Mental discipline, of course, is the major requirement when distractions intrude on focus — when ineffective performance is creating ineffective thought patterns.

When competing, a hitter must certainly limit his sight — his perspective, seeing *only* the ball. "Think small; think ball," I say to a hitter whose focus is too broad or scattered. Narrow your field of vision. Focus on the task immediately at hand.

But when assessing his performance — or his life — or his world —a hitter must hold a *fuller* view. I asked the young player I referred to above similar questions about choices, but made them problems other players might face, not issues that he himself had to deal with. He had sensible responses to all hypothetical dilemmas "outside the frame" of his life.

When all is going well in your personal and professional world, the muscles are allowed freedom of function. They celebrate your healthy **perspective** after each performance. But getting the mind right when things are not going ideally is the key to athletic excellence. Good perspective in the face of adversity qualifies as "mental toughness" — the coin of the realm for elite athletes. A poorly directed perspective, of course, can make times appear to be more difficult than they actually are.

Develop your perspective carefully.

Poor perspective is often the result of thinking you can't cope with situations you're facing or will be facing. Use your brain. You've handled these same situations well before. The difference isn't in the circumstance; it's in your perception of it — and of yourself. You got where you are because of your talent and your trust in it. How do you lose it? By interpreting events and consequences with a jaundiced eye.

Trust your ability to cope with whatever *reality* you meet, and you'll create a healthy perspective. That, in turn, will encourage self-confidence. As a result, your relaxed muscles will be free to give you what you want from them: a more consistently effective performance.

The fuller view is a view that allows the hitter to recognize his life and performance as it is, rather than as he wishes or needs it to be. It allows him the health of knowing reality and facing it with common sense and courage. It allows him to be rational, rather than emotional about his mistakes and shortcomings, about his goals and his results.

If you think this all sounds more like philosophy than hitting, you're right and wrong at the same time. It is part of a philosophy of hitting. Hitters will ask me if I can provide them with some relaxation techniques. "Sure," I say, "but first tell me why you're having trouble relaxing." The answers are varied, but most are related to a poor perspective, to imaginings and fears that distort their realities. It's hard to relax when you're anxious (scared?) and anticipate failure because of your point of view.

An anxious hitter feels tension in his muscles and well as in his mind. He doesn't see the ball well, of course. But to make matters worse, he jumps out at pitches, his body leaving "too early," and his bat drags through the hitting zone, instead of whipping through it. A poor outlook can do this — *has* done it to many players, many times.

You've heard how much coaches, scouts, and managers value "a good attitude?" Where does an attitude — good or bad — come from? The source is whatever perspective the player has developed. Change a bad perspective and you change a bad attitude. Hold a good perspective and you hold a healthy and valued attitude.

The hitter with an unhealthy perspective says, "This is a threat." A healthier point of view is, "This is a challenge." The former of the two says, "I can't." The latter is able to say, "I can."

The strongest statement is, "I will." But what if a hitter *does not*? Well, he'll just makes an adjustment next time. He'll ask himself the questions presented in an earlier chapter: "What was I trying to do?" "What went wrong?" "What am I going to do next time?" This, instead of making excuses or cursing his fate — or himself.

We're all products of everything that's ever happened to us. So, from our early years, we develop a perspective based on whether positive people or negative people have surrounded us. Energetic people or lazy people. People who were mentally strong or mentally weak. And so on.

But your experience doesn't have to be your fate. It may help explain why you are as you are, but if you happen to be unhappy with your attitude and perspective, you can choose to change them. Or choose not to change, in which case you become a victim of your past. You would be better served if you learn to distinguish between what is inevitable — beyond your control — and what you can choose — actions that can change your circumstance.

I'll use a pitcher to help illustrate the point, as it pertains to performance. Mike Hampton was struggling badly in his first seven starts as a member of the 2000 New York Mets pitching staff. He would be a free agent at the end of that season — and was, of course, hoping for a "good" contract.

Something happened at that point. Explained Hampton, "I just got it in my head that this is a game. There's a lot of stuff going on in the world that's a lot tougher than what I'm going through," he said. His newly gained — or rediscovered — perspective allowed him to relax, to trust his talent and — to "just pitch."

This subject is so important simply because how you interpret the world and what happens to you will dictate how you function. How you approach tasks, challenges and risks, successes and failures. It will affect, therefore, the way a hitter approaches the ball. Clear vision or clouded vision? Relaxed or tense? Does the hitter hold himself responsible or does he hold himself "at fault?" Or does he make excuses? The complete list of attitudes affected by perspective is too lengthy for these pages.

But the starting point for a healthy perspective is clear and simple. Think instead of feel. Be rational, rather than emotional. Step back (out of the frame) and use your brain. Emotions such as frustration, anger, fear, resentment, and jealousy — to name a few — distort your perceptions.

Manny Ramirez is considered by many to be the most dominant offense player in baseball. His perspective helps his natural talent. While acknowledging that hitting a baseball well is a difficult task, and difficult times result during a season, he philosophizes that good results "come and go." Ramirez says, "You can't tell which way it is going to go for you. So you just have to go with it. I'm not going to go crazy worrying about it..."

Work, rather than worry, when results are not "going for you." Focus on your approach, rather than catastrophic declarations or imaginings.

Here are three examples of ways players have revealed their poor perspective to me: "This guy has an unhittable slider." The remark was made by a Double-A hitter. My response: "If he can't be hit, why is he pitching in Double-A?"

Dave Hudgens was managing a Rookie League team in Idaho in 1985. On a road trip, Dave told a pitcher to sit next to me on the bus. The pitcher, who had quality stuff, was 1-8 at the time. "I'm going to be released because I'm losing games," he told me as soon as he sat down. My response: "Cy Young lost 316 games and they named an award after him." (The Rookie League pitcher was promoted two weeks later, though his won-lost record wasn't much better.)

"I had a terrible day today," a major league hitter with the Florida Marlins said to me in the clubhouse after a game. He had gone 1-4, walked, scored two runs, moved a runner over and hit the ball hard every at-bat, except the one during which he moved the runner to third, by putting the ball in play to the right side. My response cannot be printed here, but you must know by now (especially since you're outside the frame) that he had a good day and I explained that to him emphatically.

Rockies first baseman Todd Helton has developed a healthier perspective. The quality of his life and of his at-bats have made that very apparent. (The Associated Press voted him the 2000 season Player of the Year.) Helton told *The New York Times* writer, Ira Berkow, "When I first came up to the majors and I'd have a bad day, I'd punish myself. I would do something like not eat dinner. Now I've come to appreciate that we play 162 games a year, and you're going to have bad days. And not eating dinner hurts, doesn't help."

His hitting coach in Colorado, Clint Hurdle, did help. Helton credits his coach with developing the hitter's mental game, particularly, in Hurdle's words, that "important ability to accept failure [of a bad at-bat] and categorize it as a one-time thing." Helton's change in perspective became apparent. And his league-leading .372 batting average over the course of the 2000 season indicated that Helton didn't have too many bad days.

A very common problem is that hitters who consider themselves to have had a bad day will act out of that perspective the *next* day. They'll approach their at-bats with a sense of urgency. The ball will get "smaller"; their breathing will shorten; their muscles will get tighter. That day has a much better chance of *actually* being bad.

A 1-4 day — or an 0-5 day — won't cause the breakdown. The hitter's interpretation of the day will. It's essential to see the ball well, but first see your world, the game, and yourself clearly, accurately, objectively. By doing so you can then assess your at-bats with intelligence, and make the necessary adjustments. As a bonus, your perspective will allow your talent to be free to express itself.

But every day brings a new challenge, and the "healthiest" hitters will share the point of view of Angels outfielder Darren Erstad: "If you fail, you have to remember, 'I'm going to be OK tomorrow.'"

Erstad plays with skill — and intensity. His point of view is healthier than it was when he was younger. "My parents tell stories about how much I hated to lose when I was a kid," Erstad said. "I always hated to lose regardless of what it was, even when the family was playing Yahtzee."

Erstad's manager, Mike Scioscia, recognized an improved perspective, illustrated by Erstad's patience as a hitter. "I think he understands that every play [including at-bats] does not turn out to be life and death," said Scioscia. "He can be intense, but he is also able to let things go."

This perspective, of course, allows a hitter's approach to his next at-bat to remain aggressive, functional — and uncomplicated.

(As a matter of record, Erstad's .355 batting average in 2000 resulted from his 240 hits, the 13th highest total on the major league all-time single-season list. A fairly functional approach, we can assume.)

One of the most impressive hitters in the big leagues is Mets catcher Mike Piazza. His outlook impresses me greatly, as well. Whether questioned about salary, MVP candidacy, winning the division, the wild-card race, or any other general question — as it relates to his performance — Piazza always says the right thing. Over and over. "All I can do is [play] with a clear mind, play hard and keep things basic," he says. And other words to that effect.

"Basic." Meaning uncomplicated, immediate, controllable. See the ball; hit the ball, as you know.

REMEMBER

- A healthy perspective allows you to see your world objectively and rationally, rather than with vision clouded by emotional needs.

- A perspective on life should be *wide*, taking in all aspects of your daily life and performance.

- Identify the nature of your perspective. Ask yourself, "How do I tend to view the issues or tasks I face?" (Optimistically or pessimistically? With confidence or uncertainty? With hope or despair? Etc.)

- Work on developing a healthier perspective through this awareness.

- Trust in your ability to cope with difficulties and approach them aggressively, rather than submissively or fearfully.

- A healthy perspective encourages self-confidence and helps the muscles to be relaxed. The opposite is true of a distorted perspective, which provokes self-doubt and a sense of urgency.

- The brain is a hitter's valuable tool for building a proper perspective. Think clearly. Step back and "get out of the frame."

- A hitter's perspective should be *narrow* — limited to function and focus. (See the ball; hit the ball.)

- You have a choice to see and be what you wish. "See" with a healthy outlook; "be" with a healthy attitude.

- Know how to evaluate at-bats. Ask yourself: "Did I see the ball well?" "Did I hit it hard?" "Did I execute what I wanted to do?" If not — make adjustments based on understanding, rather than negative reaction. Know what you want to do during your next at-bat. Then trust your talent and put the last at-bat in your history book as a useful lesson.

CHAPTER 8

Routine, Ritual, and Superstitution:
Who's in Control?

"The golden opportunity you are seeking is in yourself. It is not in your environment; it is not in luck or chance, or the help of others; it is in yourself alone."

— Orison Swett Marden

The best way to start this chapter is by defining the terms in its title. **Routine** is a good word for a hitter. A routine is a set, customary course of behavior. It's an important part of preparation (a subject that will be addressed in the next chapter).

Ritual can also be a good word, implying a detailed method of procedure that is regularly followed. Faithfully followed. There's where the word can lead a hitter astray. He must have faith in himself first and in his choice of behaving consistently. Behavior he established because it *works* — in a practical way. If a ritual is followed in a compulsive way — a way which a hitter can't resist or adjust, that ritual is no longer a "good" one. Regardless of how much or how little sense it makes. The tail wags the dog.

Rituals, you see, often become obsessive, superstitious acts. **Superstition** is a belief that some action not logically related to an event (an at-bat, for example) will influence its outcome. Worse yet, the superstition is often based on a fearful, compulsive *dependence* upon that belief. Not good at all, to understate my view.

The engine of superstition is unlimited desire accompanied by limited self-trust. Francis Bacon wrote that all people have a blind side, and that side is superstition. Unfortunately, too many

61

ballplayers develop the habit. The great ones manage to do well *in spite* of superstition. Not because of it. They are the exceptions, not the rule.

Control is the final important word in the title. Let me quote the famous Serenity Prayer here:

"God grant me the serenity to accept things I cannot change, courage to change things I can and wisdom to know the difference."

To *know the difference* between what each of us can control — and what we cannot. That understanding comes from where the brain resides. It surely is not the brain that tells a hitter to kiss his bat in order to get a hit. Everyone who pays such "lip-service" to his bat would then become a great hitter.

Or perhaps, stepping on a cup in the dugout does the trick? You get the point. Then why do so many players have so many superstitions? It has do with a player trusting forces beyond himself, rather than trusting himself — and his ability. Yes, the player's brain understands this, but the body responds to the strongest message sent to it. If a player doesn't kiss his bat and thereby feels he will do poorly, his muscles will get that message. It isn't a productive one. The muscles, after all, control the bat.

During the 1998 season, when we were both with the Tampa Bay Devil Rays, I asked Wade Boggs about his rituals and superstitions. "They make me feel comfortable," he told me. "What about changing your shoes or batting gloves after a bad at-bat?" I asked. "Do you really think that's responsible for a good at-bat if one follows the change?" He was hesitant. To get to the point, this is what we established as we spoke: he had never changed his hitting approach over the course of his career. "I hit just the way I did in high school," he "confessed." That was why he was so successful!

Getting 3,000 hits indicates consistency. "Consistent behavior gets consistent performance," I tell players. Boggs — and Tony Gwynn — have been consistent in their preparation and approach to hitting. Running at 7:17 PM every night, or taking the same number of balls off a fungo in pre-game — which Boggs always did — is a ritual of preparation. It is consistent behavior. Gwynn, another 3,000-hit man, has his own **ritual** and **routine.**

To have observed the sense of purpose Boggs and Gwynn brought to batting practice is to have watched hitters with a routine that is the integral part of preparation. Nomar Garciaparra is another exemplar in that regard. Though he may irritate some observers with his antics between pitches, that behavior is not what got him the results, awards, and contract. His talent did. I'm sure he knows and trusts that.

It's disturbing to me to see players make superstitious changes or perform repetitively purposeless acts, because I worry that these players come to believe in obsessive, rather than functional behavior. Boggs and Garciaparra, as suggested earlier, are exceptions, not the rule. My great concern is for young hitters who do not trust themselves, and who act out behaviors because of fear of consequences if they don't act that way. This is certainly not the aggressive mentality elite athletes have. Nor should it be the attitude a young athlete develops. If everyone could perform the way Wade and Nomar have performed, I would stop worrying. We all know that is not the case, and, because of this truth, I know I'll continue to be concerned.

In the Johnny Mize book on hitting, the slugger tells a story about the Hall-of-Fame manager John McGraw who, Mize says, "arranged for a horse-drawn wagon of barrels to pass by the ball park as the players were entering the field." Mize explained, "Barrels are supposed to symbolize base hits and this little psychology made the players confident that they would get a barrelful that day." Did they? *That* and every day? The statistics suggest otherwise. A wonderful, simplistic, and unsophisticated story about the baseball culture more than 70 years ago. But the mentality still lingers.

The seventh and final game of the 1997 World Series went extra innings. During the 11th inning, I rose from my seat in the Marlins' dugout to get a cup of water at the cooler. Two men reached base while I stood there sipping. I turned to go back to my seat. Moises Alou grabbed my arm. "Stay right there," he said. "We've got something going." Was I responsible for Edgar Renteria's Series-winning single moments later? You'd better know better.

If hitting is all about making effective adjustments, how can a young hitter understand his approach if he tends to believe that barrels suggest *how* to get basehits, or that "same seats" in the dugout will dictate outcome, or that the wrong socks are the culprits for his hitting problem? Same answer as above.

To attribute the outcome of at-bats to compulsive or superstitious acts is to avoid taking responsibility. Yet, responsibility is one of the greatest tools in the world for shaping and developing people and giving substance to their behavior.

You can *seek* "comfort," if that's what you believe you need. Mize said that maybe "these little things give a player more assurance." (Assurance of hits?) But you'd better *take* responsibility — if you want **control**. As a player and as a person.

 REMEMBER

• A **routine** is a set and regulated behavior pattern.

• A **routine** can become a **ritual** — which is fine — so long as the **ritual** doesn't lead to obsessive or compulsive behavior.

• **Superstition** is illogical and is too often based on a subtle fear. It is therefore a hindrance to the development of an aggressive mentality.

• It is essential to know what you can and cannot **control**. Thought, attitude, and behavior can be controlled. Fate and powers beyond yourself cannot.

• To accept responsibility for your actions is to encourage the development of yourself as an effective performer and a self-actualized person.

CHAPTER 9

The Preparation Cycle

"The strength of a man's virtue should not be measured by his special exertions, but by his habitual acts."

— Pascal

In the previous chapter, the value of routine was established in general terms. Routine — set behavior — plan. Habitual acts. Call it what you will, effective preparation is grounded in such behavior.

Diet, sleeping habits and workout schedules are part of a hitter's preparation. The self-discipline required to prepare yourself *off* the field can be as formidable as what it takes *on* the field. In some cases, more formidable. Self-proclaimed "gamers" rationalize that they're *ready* when they "get between the lines." It's the excuse of those who cannot hold up under what they consider to be too much painful discipline: the discipline of conscientious preparation. They're obviously not disciples of Euripides, who wrote, "Do not consider painful what is good for you." And their "game" is far beneath the level of those who are committed to total preparation. And, for that matter, far below their own potential, whether they care to admit it or not.

Important as they are, these off-field preparations, and the related philosophy, are too inclusive for these pages. [Refer to *The Mental Game of Baseball*, Chapter 9: Preparation] If you want to get to the "big dance," you must first learn the steps. I'll stick to on-field stepping here.

But before getting to those specifics, I must again note that baseball has been called a game of adjustments. The vehicle for this adjustment is your brain. The emotional system won't allow you to *learn* from your mistakes. This has been discussed in earlier chapters. The reminder is to reiterate the point that the ability to make an adjustment implies the *ability* to learn from mistakes. The ability should allow the hitter to apply his learning. He's prepared for the next pitch, or the next at-bat, or the next game.

Hitting in "the cycle."

The cycle of preparation is as follows:

- You learn.
- You apply the learning in batting practice.
- You assess your approach during BP and make necessary adjustments.
- You bring those adjustments into the game.
- You learn from the game performance and make further necessary adjustments in the next practice. (These changes can be physical or mental.)

I frequently address the word "normal" when talking to professional athletes. Players tend to excuse their occasional counterproductive preparation (laziness, lack of effort, lack of concentration, etc.) as "normal." I tell them that "normal" is the excuse of the normal — meaning the mediocre. The players who succeed are those who behave with *exceptional* mental discipline. They are the players who are preparing to be extraordinary and whose efforts and applications make them **winners**.

BATTING PRACTICE

Use batting practice or it will use you. (Remember the question in the previous chapter: Who's in control?) You've heard the time-worn homily, "Practice doesn't make perfect; perfect practice makes perfect." It may be tedious, but it's true, used and re-used the way a good book is read and re-read. But it's meaningless

— unless you integrate its truth into your behavior. A careless batting practice will produce a hitter who suddenly cares — during the game — and has not readied himself for competition. BP has used him — always poorly in such cases. Someone once said that people seem to save themselves for the Senior Prom, but they forget that somewhere along the line, they'd better learn to dance.

Learn to hit — and keep learning. *Have a **purpose** for everything you do in batting practice*. If you're having trouble seeing the ball, use some pitches just to track the ball. Let the coach throwing BP know what you're doing. Such behavior is unconventional, and many players are afraid to do that. But the great athletes aren't afraid to stand out or be different. They do what's *necessary* in order for them to improve and be ready to compete.

Practice going the other way. Look for pitches away. Montreal manager Felipe Alou raves about Expos outfielder Vladimir Guerrero's batting practice. "The first round, he hits *everything* to right field," says Alou. (Alou's emphasis on "everything.")

Take bad pitches! (Swinging at every pitch is another way of being used by BP. You wouldn't do that during a game.) Simulate counts in your mind. Simulate game situations, such as moving a runner over or driving one in. If this is part of the team's BP plan, beware. It becomes so familiar to you that you may "just go through the motions." Have intense focus always! Take every pitch seriously. You will in the game, so you must in practice — if excellence is your goal.

Item: In the 2000 National League Divison Series, Will Clark hit a first-inning, three-run homer off Atlanta's Tom Glavine to lead the St. Louis Cardinals to a three-game sweep of the Braves. After the game, manager Tony LaRussa had this to say about the veteran first baseman: "Will Clark could have taken an 0-for-4 today. It makes no difference in his approach. Will gets himself ready for this competition. He's competing at the highest level you can get to. Today, he was typical Will. Clark was competing and trying to do something important," LaRussa continued. "He prepared himself to have a great at-bat."

That preparation is consistent for Clark and every hitter who aspires to be exceptional. They are not casual about their at-bats. They take control of what they can, in this case their approach, which is part of their preparation. [See Chapter 11]

Do whatever is necessary as you learn more about yourself as a hitter. I've said in a previous chapter that you'll be the most important coach you'll ever have. Be the most effective one, as well.

GAME TIME

There are seven "situational stations" for a hitter's preparation during a game: the dugout, the on-deck circle, the walk to the box, the batter's box, the area just outside the box, inside the batter's box, and the dugout again.

1) Dugout

In the dugout, a hitter should be attentive to the opposing pitcher: his pitches, his tendencies, his strengths, and apparent weaknesses. The hitter should watch how his teammates handle the pitcher; which approaches are successful, which unsuccessful. And know why. A pitcher's tendency to throw a particular pitch on a particular count will not necessarily be an absolute, but it can be helpful, especially earlier in the count or on a hitter's count.

Notice the pitcher's release point. Does he change it? If so, when? Watch everything that's going on. Not only does the mental energy you spend provide information to prepare you, it also enhances your concentration skills. That is part of a winner's preparation. Like running and lifting. In this case, mental stretching for stamina.

2) On-Deck Circle

The on-deck circle is the spot for reviewing whatever mechanical keys you use. For example, "Stay back." Or something related to body balance. Whatever your need is.

Take some practice swings, timing the pitcher. Mark McGwire

stands and has, essentially, a practice at-bat in terms of timing. Loosen your muscles, ready your mind. Watch the delivery. Follow the ball.

Before the 2000 season, Colorado hitting coach Clint Hurdle asked Todd Helton to focus at a higher level, telling him to be locked into his at-bat from the time he left the dugout, metaphorically allowing the pitcher "no room to breathe."

Helton, in fact, doesn't hang out in the on-deck circle. He waits closer to homeplate, stares at the pitcher, hoping to put himself in the pitcher's peripheral view — and head.

3) En Route to the Batter's Box

Assess the game situation. Do you want to move a runner over from second? Is there a man on third with one out or none out? What ball location do you want in order to get the job done? What pitch? Have your plan formulated before you reach the box.

Says Hurdle, "I firmly believe that a lot of at-bats are determined before you get in the box. I firmly believe you can empower a pitcher at times by your body language and how you react to certain situations."

In other words, bring a focused and assured competitor to the box, not a reluctant victim. Whatever your state of mind, get whatever edge you can by taking on the posture of a warrior. The better your body language, the better chance your muscles have of doing their job.

4) Outside the Batter's Box (before stepping in)

One more reminder of your mechanical cue. Take a deep breath in and exhale. You're letting the carbon dioxide — the muscle inhibitor — out. More pure oxygen — the muscle enhancer — remains. Such breathing will help you be more relaxed.

Houston shortstop Tim Bogar had a 12-for-36 stretch over 10 games during the 2000 season. He had been hitting under .200 before that period. His hitting coach, Harry Spilman, worked with him on being more aggressive — and being more relaxed at the same time. The bat won't be quick and aggressive through the hitting zone unless the muscles are relaxed. Cue yourself to "be easy."

5) In the Batter's Box

Get into the box with a clear head. The only message you should hear from your inner voice is, "See the ball." Again, "Be easy." If you're thinking about mechanics, or anything else for that matter, get out of the box. Your attention will be divided; the ball will look small and your reaction will be slow.

6) Outside the Box (between pitches or after calling "time")

If your mind is cluttered, and if you've taken a pitch or swung and missed (or fouled it off), step back out of the box and fix your thinking pattern. If, before the pitch, you have time —call "time." Coach yourself with the reminder, "Just see the ball." Another deep breath and get ready to see the ball and hit it. If all is well, and you're just thinking "ball," tell yourself, "Stay right there."

7) Back in the Dugout (after an at-bat)

Whatever the results, whenever you get back into the dugout, review your at-bat. If you're satisfied with your approach, irrespective of the result, leave it alone. If you're unhappy with it, ask yourself the three questions and answer them: "What was I trying to do?" "What went wrong?" "What do I want to do next time?" Then leave it alone. You're prepared. If anger and frustration come back to the dugout with you, vent it. Purge yourself. You're allowed 15 to 20 seconds. *Then,* ask and answer those questions — and move on. Get your head back into the game.

If you retain your frustration and anger, urgency and anxiety will set in. You will have prepared yourself for another unacceptable at-bat. You will have responded poorly to your at-bat. Your next approach will suffer because of it. Remember, a good response to a bad at-bat will help keep your approach consistent. Consistently good.

A later chapter will deal with "confidence." The one thing you can always be confident in — and control — is your preparation. The most confident hitters are always ready — always prepared.

1) DUGOUT - OPP. PITCHER
2) ON DECK - MECHANICS, TIME PITCHER
3) ENROUTE TO BOX - GAME SIT. / COACH
4) OUTSIDE BOX - DEEP BREATH
5) IN BOX - CLEAR HEAD, "COMPETE"
6) BETWEEN PITCHES - STEP OUT, ADJ. IF NEEDED
7) AFTER AB - TRYING TO DO?
    WHAT WENT WRONG?/RIGHT?
    NEXT TIME
    GOOD RESPONSE TO BAD AT BAT

BREATHE!

 **REMEMBER**

- Preparation is readiness.
- The best hitters know how to make necessary adjustments to their approaches. The best learners make the best adjustments.
- You learn from your practices as well as from your game at-bats.
- The application of learning with disciplined batting practice rounds is the preparation for success.
- Your goal should be to behave exceptionally, rather than excusing inappropriate preparation as "normal."
- Establish a batting practice routine in which there is a sense of purpose for everything you do.
- Understand and review the seven specific game-time "stations" noted above.
- Integrate that understanding into behavior through mental discipline. You will then be able to trust your preparation, and thereby enhance your confidence.

CHAPTER 10

Relax the Mind:
Relax the Muscles

"When we are unable to find tranquility within ourselves, it is useless to seek it elsewhere."
— La Rochefoucauld, *Maxims*

Leading by one stroke in the final round of the 2000 Bell Canadian Open, Tiger Woods executed a shot that was said to require "boldness and brilliance." Woods, in a fairway bunker, 218 yards from the pin, with water on the front and right sides of the green, hit a 6-iron that cleared the water, flew over the flag, and stopped just off the green, 18 feet from the hole.

Grant Waite, Woods's playing partner, was duly impressed. Shocked, as well. "Amazing," he said. "To have the mind-set, the calmness in his body to hit that shot, is the advantage he has over other players."

Boldness. Brilliance. And tranquility within.

Woods's own response: "It's a thrill to see what you have *inside*...Sure, I get nervous, but I know how to handle it...*You focus everything on what you're doing.* [My emphasis in each sentence.] It was a lot of fun."

He was relaxed and he was aggressive. And focused on task, not himself or consequences.

Australian Olympic super swimmer, 17-year-old Ian Thorpe: asked about pressure: "It doesn't weigh me down, it pushes me forward." He is motivated, he said, not burdened; challenged, not threatened.

Threats, pressures, and "I have-to's" all inhibit a relaxed state for a hitter — or anyone else. The perceptions create a state of excitement and/or anxiety that causes tension and an accompanying inability to perform effectively. A healthy perspective [See Chapter 7] will best enable a hitter to have a relaxed state of mind and muscle ("tranquility within…"). But, in the *absence* of such a point of view, the anxious hitter should utilize essential techniques that will help him cope and perform.

Some players think that relaxing means forfeiting aggressiveness. My response to them: "I'm talking about relaxing the muscles, not the focus. I can care and still be relaxed. I can be intense without being tense."

Item: Angels hitting coach Mickey Hatcher said of Troy Glaus before the slugging third baseman's 2000 season had barely begun: "Glaus needs to be relaxed, but he can still be aggressive. When he can separate and figure out the two, there's no telling what he can do."

Glaus seems to be learning. His 2000 final production: .284 BA, 47 HR, 102 RBI — and 112 bases on balls. (He's not all the way there yet: 163 K's.)

When a hitter indicates to me that he cannot relax, my first attempt is to help him gain a better perspective about his "predicament." [Again, Chapter 7 must be referred to here.] The cause of his anxiety is the problem; the tension is the symptom. Solve the problem and the symptom disappears. This takes an effort of will, and it is an arduous and on-going process.

While working on the solution to the problem, the hitter should utilize specific techniques that address the symptom. Relaxation techniques.

First consideration: **Awareness**. Recognize the state of arousal. I liken a high state of excitement to an inner flame that is out of control. "You'll burn your house down," I tell players who are aroused to that level. On the other hand, a player whose arousal is too low (complacent, disinterested) I tell, "You're flickering; the flame is going out." What I ask for is "heat and light." (Balance. Aggressiveness under control!) The proper and very individual level of arousal that best serves each hitter. He must learn this by experimentation if he hasn't acquired it yet.

Most hitters are all-too-aware of their tensions, but they aren't as aware of the **techniques** for addressing them. That's step two: the hitter should find out what works best for him.

Breathe or die.

That's one of my admonitions to players who I see holding their breath during times of tension. An essential technique for addressing tension of the moment is to breathe deeply. When an audience is viewing a "scary" movie at a theater, the heightened moment that induces the scare usually causes a collective holding of breath. When the impact moment/act (say, an ax striking the victim) is completed, and the scene cuts away to a calm, pastoral setting, an audible gasp can be heard in the room. The tension is released because of an external factor.

Hitters must learn to release tension by internal means. They can't count on the outside world to take care of their needs. They should become conscious of the importance of breathing deeply — *before the moment of impact* (the next pitch). A regular pattern — part of the preparation cycle [See Chapter 9] — should be established.

Florida Marlins outfielder Cliff Floyd, *in the batter's box*, employs an excellent breathing routine, taking a good exhale as he settles his hands into hitting position. This is very fine, but hitters should *at least* take the time for a long exhale *before* they step into the box.

So, before a hitter steps into the batter's box, he should:
- Inhale. Long and slowly.
- Hold onto the breath for a short duration (three seconds?).
- Release the air slowly and naturally without "pushing" it out.
- Extend the duration of the exhale a bit, because it is the exhale that gets rid of the carbon dioxide in the blood

system and allows the oxygen to "take over." Carbon dioxide acts like a brake; oxygen an accelerator. [See Chapter 13 — "TRYING"]

Without releasing his tension, the hitter will grip the bat tightly. You've heard coaches tell hitters, "You're going to squeeze the wood out of the bat." The arm muscles tighten and the bat, when swung, drags through the hitting zone. A relaxed hitter whips the bat through the zone.

Send appropriate messages to muscles.

Chapter 5 dealt with self-talk. Its relevance to relaxation — or tension — should be clear, but begs inclusion here. The language and tone you use when speaking to yourself will help determine the state your muscles will be in.

Examples:
"What's *wrong* with you?" (frustration)
"You stink!" (self-degradation)
"Get it right!" (anger without direction)
"This guy is unhittable." (defeatism)
"I can't..." (basic negativism)
"Here we go again." (negative self-fulfilling prophecy)
"Why me?" (self-pity)
And so on.

All of the above are examples of language (and attitudes) of maladjustment. A giving in. Quitting. They induce tension, rather than relaxation, because situations are faced with no direction, no aggressiveness, no self-control, no confidence. No chance. The muscles get the message — and act accordingly.

Being positive, I tell the players, will help starve the monster. Being negative feeds it.

What helps produce a relaxed state are the very basic, positive, task-oriented directives delivered in a calm (inner and/or outer) tone of voice. Example: "Look for the ball away; be easy; track it and whack it." Again, the solutions can be briefly stated, though the problems can seem endless.

Stretch the muscles.

Tension is released by stretching the muscles. Moving (shrugging/rolling) the shoulders before getting into the batter's box helps. In between pitches, if tension is still there, step out and do it again (accompanied by calm, effective self-talk). The smoother the movement, the better. By focusing on the feeling of release in the muscles, the hitter can also keep his mind off whatever is causing the tension. Body awareness will pre-empt negative situational attention.

Out of the box, the hitter can tense his muscles, then let go — release — so he can feel the difference, the freeing up. He should also use this time to be attentive to something meaningless — his shoe top or a stone near homeplate. This helps clear the mind and allows the muscles to relax, because there is no tension-inducing significance to the focus.

The muscles in the face can also tighten. You see players opening their mouths wide and "stretching their faces." (Yankees outfielder Paul O'Neil comes immediately to mind.) It helps, especially when a hitter is aware of clenching his jaw and grinding his teeth.

Practice away from the field.

Learning how to induce a relaxed state can be worked on away from the field of battle. **Visualizing** past successes in big situations helps a hitter remind his muscles of their capability. Some big league players don't understand what visualization is. They think it's a complicated "off-the-wall" technique. My explanation is that it is simple memory in pictures. "When your head hits the pillow at night, spend five minutes recalling in your mind the kick-butt games you've had in the past. See yourself swinging, making contact. Feel how free your muscles were." They tell me they can do that. Have done that. "Then you're visualizing," I say, "Now make sure you conjure up positive images, rather than negative ones."

A number of big league players involve themselves in yoga or meditation classes. Some involve themselves in the martial arts. Former big league pitcher Dave Stewart, who gained a black belt, recognized the contribution this discipline made to his effective breathing patterns. As have many others.

For meditation, players may use tapes with soothing voices and messages — or sounds from rain forests or surf. They may just deliver positive, empowering messages to themselves in a whispery voice.

Example: "Relax. You are only conscious of silence you create within. You hear only these words. Just relax. Breathe deeply. Listen to the waves against the shore. Hear the gulls..." And so on. A relaxed state is encouraged and induced. (Needless to say, this type of exercise is not done during competition.) But the ability to listen to one's inner voice, and the ability to create messages that relieve tension, rather than creating or exacerbating it, has been enhanced.

Still others have practiced what Dr. Laurence Morehouse calls "belly breathing." In his fine book, *Maximum Performance*, he explains:

"Sitting in a chair, put your hands on your belly. As you inhale, note whether your belly is rising or falling. It should be rising, but it often isn't because when we're tense we harden the stomach muscle as though in anticipation of a blow. If your belly isn't rising as you inhale, make a conscious effort to change the pattern. Continue monitoring your breathing for at least a minute by feeling the rise and fall of your belly.

"Movement of any kind further reduces tension. Tapping the foot unconsciously; yawning and stretching; going through the motions of swinging [a bat]...motorize tension and help erase it."

Morehouse speaks of unconscious movement. My appeal to players is to be *conscious* — aware — of the techniques for helping to produce a relaxed state — and to practice these behaviors away from the field, the easier to enact them on the field. I encourage them to take account of the degree of their tensions; the situations that provoke them; the legitimacy of their perceptions;

the ability to counter them. A tension inventory, Morehouse calls it. Knowing what he's up against better enables a warrior to prepare himself and combat the enemy.

It always gets back to perspective, I feel. "Nothing can intimidate you without your consent," I tell hitters. "See things for what they are — possibility — rather than what you hope they won't be — frustration and failure. Think impending threat and disaster and you'll feel it," I say. "Change your thinking. Simplify. Think function; feel a sense of purpose. Identify what you want to do and focus on *it*. Enjoy the moment."

A healthy perspective is the best assurance of a relaxed state of mind — and muscle. It requires attention. Pudge Rodriguez, himself a good hitter, approached his Texas teammate, Raphael Palmeiro, about his approach to at-bats. What did Rodriguez want to know about? How Palmeiro could be so free of tension. "He's just so relaxed," Pudge said admiringly.

In addition to attention, the ability to relax requires due diligence.

 REMEMBER

- Muscles need assistance from the mind if they are to be relaxed.
- A relaxed state does not imply a complacent one — a non-aggressive one. Being intense without being tense is your goal.
- Perspective will dictate an initial mental assessment of a situation (at-bat). A poor perspective — one that anticipates threatening consequences — will induce tension: shortness of breath, loss of focus, tight muscles. A healthy perspective will conjure up challenge and boldness, which encourages a relaxed, aggressive, focused state, and approach.
- Self-awareness is prerequisite to addressing tension and the level of arousal which you're at — and the one you wish to attain.
- Effective breathing is essential for relaxing yourself. Formulate a routine that works best for you, using the suggestions outlined previously.
- What you say to yourself is "heard" by your muscles. Help them work for you. Let them hear appropriate language (positive and task-specific) and tonality (calm and assuring).
- Movement helps free up muscles. Get out of the box (away from the place of tension); swing the bat; shrug your shoulders; bend at the waist; "stretch your face."
- Work with relaxation exercises away from the ballpark, if necessary. This will help you improve your ability to adapt them to situational needs during competition.
- Understand that tension is most often caused by your interpretation of the external environment. The internalizing of your relaxation techniques will certainly help to fix the problem. But a healthier interpretation (*perspective*, I had to say it again!) will help you avoid it.

CHAPTER 11

Approach, Result, Response:
What Can and Cannot Be Controlled

"Know what you're doing and you'll be a confident boy. Know how to deal with what happens to you and you'll be a confident man."

— Mac Dorfman, my father

Preparation and poise. Approach and response. That was the theme of one of the many homilies my father offered me when I was a young boy. Know what you want to do; know how to do it; know how to react to whatever results. Hitters heed: how you go about your business and how you react to what happens to you both are, theoretically, within the boundaries of your control. *What* happens to you (results) are not.

Learn the difference — and learn how to manage what you are allowed to manage. Earlier on, my father had me read Rudyard Kipling's poem, *If*. It begins with the lines, "If you can keep your head when all about you / Are losing theirs..." (That was the quote at the head of Chapter 4.)

The poem ends, "If you can fill the unforgiving minute / With sixty seconds' worth of distance run, / Yours is the Earth and everything that's in it, / And — which is more — you'll be a Man, my son!"

My father's concern — and Kipling's major one, very apparently — was with behavior in every kind of circumstance. Approach and response. I've learned to share that concern, in my personal and professional life.

When dealing with hitters, I make the point early and often: the test of their efficacy will be the manner in which they deal with perceived needs, frustration, and failure to get the results they desire (statistics, the prime example). But for the sake of order, let's deal with first things first.

APPROACH:

A hitter's mental approach, believe it or not, incorporates his outlook on life and himself. [See Chapter 7] By this I mean that, to a significant extent, how he sees the ball will be influenced by how he sees the world. Let me be more specific.

The healthier a hitter's perspective is, the more secure he feels in his ability to deal with adversity — on and off the field. He'll be more confident in himself — as a person and as an athlete. This, in turn, enhances his ability to have a clear mind when approaching *any* task. It allows him to prepare with commitment and enthusiasm. It allows him to focus without external distraction (on the ball, in the hitter's case), to be aggressive, rather than tentative, to utilize his brain (understand game situation), rather than his emotions (distracted from purpose and task).

That said, let's identify what has shown itself to be an effective approach for a hitter.

1) *Situational/Functional Preparation:* The dugout and on-deck routine [keys for mechanics; See Chapter 8]. The hitter knows what he wants to do during the at-bat, what he wants to do in the particular game situation (move the runner over?); what pitch he may be looking for (not "guessing," but anticipating — with the restraint to lay off what he doesn't want); what location (where in the hitting zone); etc.

2) *Breathing:* Long, deep exhale before stepping into box. [See Chapter 10]

3) *Self-talk:* Reiterate individually developed mental keys before stepping in box. When in the box, just (say) "See the ball; be easy."

Item: Garret Anderson had very respectable results for his efforts in the 2000 season. But his focus was on his approach. "I have a checklist of things that I go through to make sure I have the right approach," the Anaheim outfielder said.

The approach is entirely within the hitter's control. This you should (must) understand. The implication is clear: you are capable of doing what it takes.

RESULTS:

Results ("stats") cannot be controlled. Refer again to the anecdote in Chapter 3 (relating to result goals) about the hitter who had 12 great at-bats (approaches) and took an o-fer the series. He controlled his frustration throughout the three-game series, and he was thereby able to control his impeccable approach. Certainly, he was unhappy about the results. But he knew — intellectually — that he had no control over where his well-hit line drives were going. [See Chapter 3, the Thoma and Conine anecdotes]

I greeted Kevin Millar, of the Florida Marlins, during a reunion, of sorts, during the 2000 season. He was not playing regularly, to say the least. He knew he had no control of the lineup card, but his frustration led him to ask me for a key he should use. "Be ready while you wait; keep it simple when you're in there."

Days later a reporter confronted Millar about his upcoming opportunity to DH against Tampa Bay. Millar said he would take a simple approach at the plate: each at-bat would be treated as if he were a pinch hitter, the duty he had been exclusively performing for some time now.

The results that night were indicative of Millar's abilities as a hitter. His effective approach had given his talent a chance to express itself. (Two for three, including a bases-loaded triple.)

Item: When Derek Jeter was struggling early in the 2000 season, he explained what was happening to him. "Sometimes the results aren't what you want," the Yankees shortstop said. "You start jumping at the ball when pitchers pitch you a certain way. You start to do something to compensate and you wind up screwing up, instead of taking the same approach every day. It has more to do with the results not being there."

Item: Braves catcher Javy Lopez is said to know why his results are poor during spells in the midst of a season. Writer Bill Zach heard that Lopez "focuses on his batting average and production numbers with the same intensity a card counter studies a deck of cards."

Lopez "admits to wanting so much to boost his numbers... that he's swinging at everything." Focusing on a future result he cannot control vs. having an approach that addresses the task of the moment — and letting the results take care of themselves. And what does "swinging at everything' suggest? Not seeing anything.

This behavior is typical of hitters who want something to happen but who forget how to *make* it happen. It takes a great amount of mental discipline. It takes trust in one's talent. But the numbers will never come to a hitter who is focusing on them. He will get results (an uncontrollable end) through an appropriate approach (a controllable means to the end).

Chris Carmichael has been Olympic champion Lance Armstrong's longtime cycling coach. He is adamant in his belief that psychological strength is the key to successful racing. One of his particular views relates to results. Says Carmichael, "It is important to set goals beyond winning and losing, because even the most talented racers will lose more often than they win." Javy Lopez and others (readers included) take note. He could just as well be talking about hitting.

RESPONSE:

Here we come to what I believe to be the key to all of our mental lives: how we respond to the events and circumstances around us. Former Cy Young Award winner (1990) Bob Welch has done a now often-imitated and exaggerated imitation of me. Says Welch, "If you tell Harvey you just murdered somebody, he'll say (here Welch throws up his hands), 'What are we going to do about it?' "

The point is accurate. What we're left with *after* an event or circumstance is our response to it. Will it be emotional and out of control? Will it be intelligent and purposeful? Will it help? Will it provide a solution? Or will it exacerbate the problem? Will it incite further emotionality from those around us?

What is appropriate? If understanding and action are required, we would want to be thoughtful and effective. If all we're required to do is hear the bad news, we're permitted the luxury of expressing our emotions, whether it be disappointment or grief or anger. But if we're called upon to act in behalf of others and/ or ourselves, we are responsible to know how to act — and we should be able to perform that action effectively.

The ability to respond appropriately is hinged on perspective and self-control. Mental health (understanding) and mental discipline (courage). Speaking for myself, I'll say it's a life's work in the development. We don't always pass the test.

As it relates to you, the hitter, responses should focus on the three questions cited earlier in the book. After a bad at-bat (approach), ask yourself, "What was I trying to do?" "What went wrong?" "What do I want to next time?" That's it! Simple and clear. Rational and intelligent. Ready for the next at-bat (part of preparation).

Throwing helmets and bats after a poor at-bat is an immature behavior, regardless of who does it. It's often an affectation of hitters, who want others to see "how much they care." It's "eyewash," as my friend Rene Lachemann terms it. If a hitter wants to vent his frustration — purge his emotions — that's fine. I tell them to do it in a private, not public, place. "Scream in the dugout tunnel. Get rid of it. Then sit down and shut up — and ask yourself the three questions. And answer them," I have said.

That, to me, is the only appropriate response. The answers may be about mechanics; they may be about the mental approach. But the on-going cycle, I tell players, is this: "Approach, result, response; Approach, result, response. If you have a good approach and you get a bad result and you have a *good response*, what will your next approach be like?" I ask. Answer: good.

"If you have a good approach, get a bad result, and have a *bad response* — what happens to your next approach?" Most likely answer: bad.

So your goal should be to keep the approach and response good — and trust that your talent will provide a good result, whether in the short or long run. The desired focus should be on the very things you *can control*, rather on than those things you cannot. It is your choice.

You can control your thoughts, emotions, and behaviors; you cannot control the world beyond you.

 **REMEMBER**

• The healthier your perspective is, the better your approaches and response will be.

• Your approach to hitting and life circumstances is within your control.

• Your responses to at-bats and the circumstances of your life are within your control. You can choose to respond emotionally or rationally. Effectively or ineffectively.

• A result is something that has already happened and is beyond your control. Or it is a desired outcome that is not within your control, whether you get what you want or do not.

• You can influence results by approaching tasks and responding to circumstances effectively.

• An effective approach includes the appropriate mental and/or physical preparation applied to tasks and situations.

• The first element of a good response is the rational and clear understanding of what has happened and how to deal with it effectively.

• The ultimate good response is the integration of that understanding into appropriate behavior — on or off the baseball field.

• Your approaches and responses are matters of choice: yours.

CHAPTER 12

Confidence and Capacity

"As is our confidence, so is our capacity."
— William Hazlitt, *Characteristics*

Hazlitt's point, made by the writer in 1823, still applies in this new millennium. And it applies to hitters, though Hazlett certainly didn't have them in mind when he expressed his view.

A lack of confidence shrinks a person to a diminished expression of his capacity as a human. It shrinks a hitter to a fraction of his capacity as a performer.

Confidence is an attitude. It can't be taught. It doesn't "*come to you*"; you must *take* it. The attitude you take on — or don't take on — will be tested throughout your life, on and off a playing field. Even exceptional people will fail the test occasionally, but they'll step back and assess themselves — and adjust their attitude so that it becomes an asset, rather than a liability.

Self-doubt is part of being human. A person who continues to doubt himself often does so because he thinks he "always ought to be confident," as one player told me. He's wrong. "Always" is not typically being human. We all have self-doubt. It is a matter of degree and determination.

Confidence comes to those who fight through their self-doubt, rather than giving in to it. The more persistent the fight, the more likely the victory. The more you win those battles, the greater your self-confidence becomes. The more confident you become, the more capacity you will develop to perform well. It is, as already noted, a lifelong ordeal. Most things that have value require great and sustained effort.

And that's a key to understanding "confidence." **An understanding that you must work on it, not wait for it.** That the fight, the resolve, will enhance your self-esteem and, therefore, your confidence. Your effort to have the appropriate approaches and responses will allow you to respect your *behavior*, which is entirely in your control — and the first thing you should ask of yourself.

Todd Helton claims that when he first came to the big leagues he lacked confidence in critical late-game at-bats. Helton admits, "When I'd be facing a closer, someone who I knew threw really hard, I'd think, 'I'm not going to hit this guy.' But I knew my attitude had to change. And slowly it did. Now I go up thinking, 'You'd better not throw a strike.'" [See Chapter 5]

Helton has also watched a lot of film and kept a diary of pitchers and their pitches. "The more you do it," Helton says, "the more confidence you get. It's an old story, but you really have to believe in yourself, believe you can do it." His preparation and self-coaching have facilitated his belief.

If you want to be a confident hitter, you must *understand* that you can control only that which you have the capacity to control. Below is a check-list of the parts of your hitting game that you have the capacity to control.

- Daily physical and mental preparation require time, effort, and consistency. A prepared hitter already has his effective preparation to be confident in. Over the years, Tony Gwynn has trusted that more than results. Todd Helton has learned to do the same. So has every great hitter.
- Control your thoughts: Have a plan before each at-bat.
- Control your focus: See the ball.
- Control your emotions: Your feelings will get in the way of your thinking. Get your thoughts focused on the task at hand:

what you want to do and how you want to do it.

- Control your responses: Understand that good, hard contact is your goal. Respond according to your goal, not according to outcome.
- If unhappy with your approach, ask yourself the three questions after the poor at-bat: What was I trying to do? What went wrong? What do I want to do next time?
- Bring that plan to your next at-bat.
- Act with confidence, as above, and you will gain confidence because of that behavior.

In exerting the control spoken of above, you — the hitter — "have it together." That will better allow you to maximize your talent and increase your capacity. Few players can claim this achievement; it is not gained with ease. But if you achieve it, you'll be a warrior armored in self-confidence.

Item: While Seattle DH Edgar Martinez was in the one of his many "grooves," he tried to explain what happens. "It's almost like you trust your swing more," he said. "Confidence plays a big part in hitting and in hitting for power. Conditioning is very important, but I think confidence is the main thing. When you trust your swing, you expect to hit balls [well]. It's almost like a rhythm." A mental rhythm, he might have added. A happy state of mind.

One of the saddest remarks I've ever heard from a professional player came from a young man playing at the Triple-A level. He grew up hearing negative and critical judgments passed on his performance by a parent. "Constant criticism," the player said. His performance could never please that parent. "It seems like my whole life has been justifying my past and worrying about my future," he said. This from a player one step from the major leagues. Surely, he must have done something right.

I've dealt with such cases frequently: parents whose expectations for their children are unrealistic, selfish, and hurtful. How can a young player (person) develop confidence when he is subjected to incessant criticism?

Answer: He cannot. Unless that young person is old enough, wise enough, and brave enough to confront the parent and explain what's going on. I've had big league players reluctant to do that. But when they finally did it, they freed themselves — and gained confidence just from the act itself.

This, I feel, has to be presented in any treatment of the term "confidence," for the simple reason that young people are greatly influenced by parents, teachers, and coaches. For better or for worse. And if it is for worse, *somebody* had better say or do something about it.

Below are some understandings that will help you as you "go after" a confident attitude:

- Confidence ebbs and flows; it's not a constant.
- Self-doubt is normal, but exceptional people don't give in to it.
- Life-threatening consequences will not result from bad at-bats.
- Failing at a task is not the same as being a failure as a person.
- Your reach is more important than your capacity.
- Self-discipline is more important than talent, which has already been established.
- Approach and response are more important than results, which you have no control over.
- Your behavior goals are more important than the expectations of others.
- Responsibility encourages confidence; excuses encourage cowardice.
- Taking risks will stretch you; being careful or fearful will limit you.
- Coaching yourself during competition with positive, functional self-talk will build confidence; criticizing

yourself and being negative will destroy it.
- Focusing on what you want to do with an at-bat will prepare you; worrying about what the pitcher might or might not do will distract you.
- *Acting* confident helps develop an attitude of confidence. Act it enough and you'll believe in it. Belief in yourself *is* self-trust — confidence, in other words.

Patience and persistence are required. Make a choice to be dedicated to self-improvement and you have moved onto and along the path to confidence. The hallmark of confident hitters is that they take control, rather than being at the mercy of fear or fate — which can be merciless.

Mamie "Peanut" Johnson played for the Indianapolis Clowns from 1953 to 1955. She was one of three women to play Negro League baseball. Before throwing out a first pitch at a Norfolk Tides minor league game in August 2000, the licensed nurse and former engineering student at New York University gave attribution to her remarkable capacities. "If you don't have no confidence in yourself, there's no use trying," the 64-year-old "Peanut" said.

There are natural instincts and acquired instincts. I've seen confidence grow. I've seen it develop. With all due respect to Mamie Johnson, the attempt is worth making. But patience and persistence are required. Make a choice to be dedicated to self-improvement and you have moved onto and along the path to self-confidence.

The hallmark of confident hitters is that they take control, rather than being at the mercy of fear or fate — which can be merciless. Without establishing that control, "there's no use trying" to think you can be a successful hitter.

REMEMBER

• <u>Focus on task during performance,</u> rather than feelings.

• Be the hitter you want to be, rather than the one you're expected to be.

• Do <u>everything possible to prepare for performance, and take your confidence in that preparation into the game</u>.

• Be aggressive and under control.

• Be a smart hitter; know what went on and what's going on, rather than worrying about what will go on. Understand past at-bats, focus on the current one, and trust the future will be manageable when you face it.

• Trust your talent.

• Play with enthusiasm and joy.

• Increase your confidence and you increase your performance capacity.

CHAPTER 13

After-words

"The similarity of our worlds depends upon the similarity of our experience ... and language..."
— J. Samuel Bois, *Explorations in Awareness*

Below is a list of words, terms, and phrases most frequently heard by me or used by me in my dealings with hitters. They are hitters' words and hitters' concerns, and make up a great part of their similar experience and language.

Most (all?), of course, can be contextually related to the chapter topics of this book, and many have been referred to in the preceding pages. They are included here because they are so frequently brought up in conversations I've had with players — as seemingly independent concerns or issues. So, it seems fitting to give these terms the emphasis and clarity of specific identification, definition, and discussion.

These terms/subjects are accompanied by commentary, anecdote, and/or explanation. They appear in alphabetical order.

ADVERSITY
"Anyone can hold the helm when the sea is calm." (Publilius Syrus)

Adversity: how fitting that this word tops the list. Adversity is what tests the mental make-up of us all. I still recall — and use — the words my father expressed when, as a bed-ridden child, I complained about my plight. "Suffering's good for you, kid — as long as you survive it." I survived it.

Every hitter suffers — sooner or later. I always tell young

players that I hope it's sooner — when they are the most resilient and the least "spoiled" by constant success. The key is to trust your talent and trust your approach. That trust will keep you from losing your head — from changing your stance every day (after every at-bat?). "This too shall pass," I'd tell my own children during difficult times.

Trusting *is* doing something about it. For a hitter, it's staying with what has always worked in the past. Minor adjustments are often made by a hitter, but major changes based on frustration or panic are counter-productive. And likely to put the hitter deeper in the depths of his ineffectiveness. [See SLUMPS below]

Mike Jarvis, coaching the St. Johns University basketball team, said about his players, "We're tough, but what I want to emphasize is that we're mentally tough. What I look for are players who have not just won all their lives, but who have been through some type of adversity and who have found a way to come through it." Good for him. Better for *them*.

Hitters talk constantly about "being uncomfortable." They should not be seduced by the "feeling" of comfort. ***Behavior*** is the key, and it is when faced with adversity — situations or "slumps" [see reference below] — that we are all most in touch with what is the greater value to us: being given what we want or working persistently and effectively to *get* what we want.

Baseball won't develop character, but adversity in the game will surely reveal it. To develop yourself as a hitter and a person, you must face difficulty with intelligence and courage. Many in the game call it "character," and I've heard managers, coaches, and scouts say "character is destiny." It might serve you as well to invert the thought. Your destiny is also your character. Adversity will test you — and reveal you.

BODY LANGUAGE

People can't know for certain what you're thinking. Your internal world is your own, unless you choose to share it. Sometimes, however, it's shared without the intention — without a word being spoken. Your body often gives pretty clear hints of what is going on inside your head.

A hitter would never think of revealing his frustration, confusion, or lack of confidence by speaking of it to an opponent. But his body can send the message without a word being said. We all recognize body signals. So even if you feel vulnerable, act invulnerable. It's a tough act, to be sure. But the more you're aware of the messages you give off when you shake your head after a bad call by the umpire, or drop your shoulders after a swing and a miss, or rage after an inside pitch knocks you off the plate — or drag a defeated-looking hitter up to the plate, the better chance you have of fixing that tendency — and acting like an effective competitor.

Says Clint Hurdle, Colorado Rockies hitting coach, "I firmly believe that a lot of at-bats are determined before you get in the box. I firmly believe you can empower a pitcher at times by your body language and how you react to certain situations...Don't let them see you sweat. Don't let them think you're bothered..."

Empower *yourself*. Act like a warrior and you have a better chance of becoming one.

CLUTCH HITTER

A clutch hitter is one who gets the job done when it is most important to have it done. How can you become one? By developing the habit of treating every at-bat as important and significant, none bigger than the one you're facing at the time. By not making distinctions, you become consistent in your approach, so that whether the game is on the line or the at-bat has little game significance, your behavior is impeccable. [See GIVING AWAY AT-BATS below]

A hitter who cauterizes the emotions of a high moment and maintains his energy during low moments always addresses the task of hitting as significant but not urgent. So he is always focused and relaxed. And that's what a hitter wants to be: intense in his vision of the ball, relaxed ("easy") in his muscles.

The hitters I've dealt with who have had difficulty in so-called "clutch" situations have put enormous significance into the at-bat, thereby tightening themselves and distracting themselves by thinking about the result, rather than their approach. You've read about this earlier, but it should be reiterated over and over to yourself. The passion of the moment will deprive you of the divine coldness of undivided attention to task. ("He's cool under pressure.")

In a post-season article in *The Sporting News*, New York Mets second baseman Edgardo Alfonzo was featured with the big headline, "**Mr. Clutch**." Teammates and opposing pitchers spoke glowingly about Alfonzo's ability to come through in big situations. Alfonzo's own remarks about that ability? "I just try to do the best I can, put the ball in play." A simple explanation of a simple approach.

By developing a consistent, simple approach, you'll be better when "the heat is on" because you won't feel the heat. Take a deep breath; get in the box; see the ball and be easy. Every time. That's part of "doing your job."

FEAR OF SUCCESS

Many players understand fear of failure, but few recognize a problem that has the same symptoms. The fear of success is based on an inability of accepting the perceived responsibility of *always* being counted on. First, the perception is unrealistic as it exists in the hitter's own mind — and does not exist in the minds of others.

Enos Cabell was a fine hitter for the Houston Astros in the '70s who announced to whomever was listening that he didn't want to be an All-Star player. "Then they'll expect too much from me," he said.

Jeff Musselman was a talented young pitcher with the Toronto Blue Jays. He is now a successful business administrator (Harvard degree) and a recovered alcoholic. "I only drank heavily after I'd performed well," he acknowledges. "I said to myself, 'They're going to expect me to do that again.' I couldn't handle the concept of my being successful. I was fine after I'd done poorly."

Years ago, a first baseman at the minor league level came over to me before a game and asked to talk. "Listen," he said. "Is there such a thing as fear of success? I know there's fear of failure."

I told him there was such a "thing" and asked if he thought he had that issue. This was his story:

When he was in high school, his coach and others told him he had "no chance of getting a college baseball scholarship." He got one.

When he was a senior in college, his coach told him he had "no chance of being drafted." He was, by Oakland.

During his early years in the minors, coaches and managers told him that he "was not a [big league] prospect."

I asked him why he was bringing this up to me now. "Well," he said. "I was hitting great [at the Double-A level], and two weeks ago the farm director came up to me and told me I'm a prospect. I went right into the tank. I can't even see straight up there [in the batter's box]. As soon as I started to hear that people thought I'd be successful I couldn't handle it."

He handled it much better with understanding and a better perspective and approach. Though he never got to the major leagues, he was a very respectable hitter and versatile player for years at the Triple-A level.

Once again, the nature of the problem is less significant than the ability to cope with it. But first, one must be aware of what is happening to him. A fear of success is a subtle but real issue.

GIVING AWAY AT-BATS

Nearly 20 years ago, I was talking with Bob Watson, who was Houston's first baseman at the time. I was interviewing good hitters as part of the research I was doing for *The Mental Game of Baseball.* We had a stimulating discussion. After it was over, Watson said calmly, "I wish I could have had this talk years ago."

"Hey, you've been a fine hitter over your career. You're a .300 hitter," I responded deferentially.

"I could have been .320 — or better," he said. "I wouldn't have given away so many at-bats."

Watson went on to explain that when he was younger, he'd "take part of the game off" if he'd gotten two hits his first two times up. "That would be my goal; to get two hits." (Results!) If he got them, he was satisfied — "Unless the game was on the line," he added.

I've heard similar stories many times since. The real result, of course, is that such at-bats are approached with less than optimum energy and focus. This can result from self-satisfaction (complacency) — as in Watson's case.

Or mental laziness: "It's the last week of the season; I'm tired, and we're not in the hunt." (Vince Lombardi: "Fatigue makes cowards of us all.")

Or from frustration, which makes giving away at-bats a singular example of mental collapse — a giving in.

Or lack of commitment and self-discipline, which is synonymous with lack of mental maturity.

Or just plain lack of understanding, which means the hitter still has plenty to learn about the game and himself.

Make every at-bat count. The expended effort and self-discipline will serve you in all aspects of your game — and your life.

Writer Nikos Kazantzakis wrote, "God makes us grubs, and we, by our own efforts, must become butterflies." [See RELENTLESSNESS below]

RIGHT?, WRONG?, LEARN!

GOOD AT-BATS

Did you see the ball well? Did you hit the ball hard? Yes? Then you had a good individual at-bat.

Did you accomplish what you wanted to accomplish in the game situation? Yes? Then it was a very good at-bat.

Todd Helton was asked about his performance after a game in August 2000, in which he'd gone 1-4. His batting average *dropped* to .397, but his night included a run-scoring groundout and a sacrifice fly. He told a questioning reporter, who wanted to pursue Helton's "quest" to hit .400, "If you get the job done, it's considered a good at-bat." End of discussion.

HITTER'S COUNT/PITCHER'S COUNT

Inappropriate self-talk induces tension — a sense of urgency. [See Chapter 10] An irony I've come across regularly is the fact that many hitters, in so-called hitter's counts, are worse off than they are in so-called pitcher's counts. Their expectations and sense of responsibility when the count is 2-0 or 3-1 blind them and tense up their muscles. They say things such as, "This is it. I gotta do it here." They "*try*" to do too much, [See TRYING, below] because of the perception that this is the time they "can do damage." Meaning, this is the time the pitcher is most vulnerable. True, but unfortunately the advantage is forfeited by the hitter's point of view, which thereby makes *him*, the hitter, more vulnerable.

In a hitter's count, you can look for a pitch in a particular area and react to it aggressively, but while *under control.* Disciplined. Too may hitters tell themselves, "I'm hacking here." Interpret that as meaning: "I'm hacking at *anything*." So they're less likely to see the ball well. Much less likely. It isn't a "now or never" count. No urgency; just a count that puts the pitcher at a disadvantage — in his own mind. What's in the hitter's mind will determine whether he can capitalize on the circumstance of count. There is no sin in going 3-0 from a 2-0 count. Or taking ball four in a 3-1 count.

A pitcher's count, on the other hand, again in an ironic sense, has served hitters well. I'll ask a hitter, "What's your expectation on an 0-2 or 1-2 count?" The answer is usually, "Just make good contact." (The same is true when I ask about hit-and-run situations.) So when a hitter feels that what he wants to do is easy, his muscles will be easy. He'll track the ball in order to make contact. He's not hacking away blindly.

The essential point seems, once again, to be: "See the ball and be easy." Irrespective of count. Then you always have whatever advantage there is to be had.

HOME RUNS
Item: Florida catcher Charles Johnson had this to say at the end of the 2000 season with the White Sox: "I've come to the conclusion [he really *knew* it before, but that season he confirmed it through behavior] that home runs are something you don't try to hit. When I *try* to lift the ball, it doesn't do anything. I ground out. So my mentality is just put the ball in play hard and take what the pitcher gives me." Johnson had a career-high total that season.

Item: First baseman Jeff Bagwell always claimed he's not a home run hitter. "I'm a line-drive hitter," Bagwell has said. His drives often go over the fence. In 2000 he broke his own Houston Astros record of 43 homers.

Home runs happen. [See TRYING below]

MECHANICS

Kinetic memory governs your muscles — unless there is interference from a counterproductive mental agenda. Then the muscles receive messages that cause them to tighten up ("muscle up"), lose their natural fluidity and control, and, instead, become controlled by the urgent messages imposing themselves into your thinking pattern. Leave your muscles alone! Trust them. You've been swinging a bat since you were a child. Your muscles have learned. And they are at their best when your mind does not interfere.

Batting practice is part of a daily routine on a baseball field. Thinking practice is not. Extra batting practice taken to work on a problem that doesn't exist creates the problem. A self-consciousness related to mechanics which is taken into the batter's box during the game. You'll have no chance seeing the ball if you're thinking about your hand position — or feet — or anything related to your hitting mechanics. Trust your mechanics; see the ball.

Late in the 2000 season, Charles Johnson was asked to explain his career-high batting average (.290s). "I'm just relaxing and focusing on quality at-bats. I'm letting my muscles do what they know how to do," he said. "I'm not *giving away at-bats* [see above] by worrying about mechanics. And I'm seeing the ball real well."

That's what happens. That simple — to understand. Trust is doing what you understand.

MENTAL DISCIPLINE / TOUGHNESS

These are the "labels" most frequently used to acknowledge and describe a focused and formidable competitor. To be a competitor is to be disciplined in so many ways, so I most often use the term "mental *discipline*."

My definition is short and to the point. Mental discipline is the ability to focus effectively on the task at hand, without being affected by any external or internal distractions — such as fear, pain, big-game situations, booing fans, family/personal relationships and issues, media, money — or "slumps." [See SLUMPS below] Such efficacy is discipline of the highest order. Tough to be. "Tough" in the being.

Renowned hitting coach Walt Hriniak, discussing the poor 1999 hitting performance of White Sox slugger Frank Thomas, summed it up succinctly and tactfully. "It looked like he lost some of his discipline," Hriniak said. Other observers would say Thomas had lost much of his discipline. But Thomas's disciplined approach was again in evidence during his outstanding 2000 season. [See RELENTLESSNESS below]

Phillies outfielder Pat Burrell showed in his 2000 rookie season that he is a disciplined hitter. Asked about his success hitting with the bases loaded, Burrell said the reason was simple: he knows he's going to see a pitch he can hit, so he waits for it. When he sees it, he aggressively responds. In other words, in a big situation he uses patience instead of passion.

Item: St. Louis outfielder J.D. Drew, assessing his 1999 season at the beginning of the Cardinals' 2000 spring training session: "I wasn't mentally tough enough."

Item: From *The Sporting News*, October 2, 2000: "White Sox left fielder Carlos Lee has shown much more discipline at the plate...Last week, after falling behind Detroit's Jeff Weaver 0-2, Lee shortened up his swing and wound up seeing 15 pitches before drawing a walk. It was only the second time in his career that Lee has walked after falling behind 0-2."

Item: (same source as above): "The Yankees have won three World Series championships with this offensive strategy: work the count, wait for your pitch, don't try to do too much. But when the team is struggling to buy a run, that discipline goes out the window, manager Joe Torre says. He sees his players trying to go deep [see TRYING below], to deliver the hit that will bring the team out of its funk. Of course, that's the worst thing they could be doing."

Staying with what you know works during tough times re-quires great discipline, as has been said. Such acts of will can be called "well-intentioned concentration." It's important to develop that ability, as tough as it is — which is why those who do it consistently are, themselves, mentally tough.

The key, after all is said and yet to be done: to be stronger than what may be happening inside you at a particular moment. In other words, act appropriately in spite of how you may feel. Tough it out.

PRESSURE

This is some of the counterproductive language that hitters so often use: "Gotta get this run in"; "Need a hit here"; "The game's on the line"; "The game's on my shoulders this AB"; "Now or never." And words to that effect. The effect of pressure. The effect of conjuring up dire responses (teammates, manager, fans, media, *et. al.*) if he, the hitter, "doesn't come through." The effect of the imperative (must, have to, etc.) with the "or else" consequences. Heavy stuff; the weight of self-induced pressure.

Years ago, when I was teaching a psychology class, the sub-ject of "pressure" and stress (because of problems real and imag-ined) was being discussed. I brought into class a large, empty, tin linseed oil can on the day the topic was to be treated. And an air pump. At the beginning of the class, I gave a demonstration. First, I took the cap off the opening of the can and put a rubber stopper into it. Then, the thin hose from the air pump was inserted into a hole in the stopper. The pump was to be used to extract air from the can.

Slowly I pumped the air out of the can. A crackling noise began to sound as the can's shape gradually changed. The sides were collapsing. I pumped faster; the noise became more pro-nounced and the can collapsed and shriveled. When I stopped the can's shape was completely distorted.

I asked the students what they had seen happen.

"It collapsed because of the air pressure outside," one stu-dent answered.

"It folded because there was nothing left inside," I responded emphatically.

Prior to the demonstration, we had noted that air applies 15 pounds of pressure per square inch on every surface. The pressure put on the can's external surface was 15 pounds per square inch. The pressure inside the can had been the same — until I sucked the air out of the can. Because there was no longer any air inside, to "combat" the pressure from the air outside, the can "folded."

"The same physical principal applies to us," I said to the students. "We have air inside us that keeps our bodies intact. Our psyches follow the same principle. The 'pressing' problems or issues we have all can create 'pressure.' But these issues won't 'dent' us or 'buckle' us if we have what it takes to stay whole. It takes coping mechanisms. The can's internal force is air; our internal psychological force is whatever coping mechanisms we have," I said. Though oversimplified, the point seemed clear to them.

Part of the oversimplification is that "pressure" is a perception. Refer once more to the remarks of Australian swimmer Ian Thorpe, who said pressure "doesn't weigh me down; it pushes me forward."

What one hitter will even perceive as pressure — a "threatening situation" — another hitter will see as an exciting opportunity or challenge. [See Chapter 7]

Still, if the environment truly presents difficult situations that must be dealt with, a hitter who has 'the right stuff' will survive at least, and thrive, at best, in spite of whatever external problems exist. He will cope. He will manage himself and, to that extent, "manage" his environment. He will not control the externals, but he will control the internals — thereby applying equal pressure from within. He will not cave in.

"Baseball is not pressure," Sammy Sosa has said. "Pressure is when you're seven years old, and you don't have food to eat. So when you've come from nowhere and have all that I have now, I sleep like a baby every night." Nevertheless, if someone else has decided baseball *is* pressure...well, it is. Now it must be coped with. Push back, as the air in the can did. And don't let anyone pump it out.

You'll take pride in handling difficult situations, because you can handle your emotional responses. That's mental toughness, as you remember.

RELENTLESSNESS

The players on every team I've ever worked with have heard me use a particular word as a credo. Whether alluded to on tee shirts I distributed each spring training or reiterated in talks before daily stretching, my words to players have been based on the belief that they know what appropriate behavior is during competition. The difficulty is in their acting on what they know.

Simply, they — you — must be **relentless**. Unyielding and uncompromising in the pursuit of *consistently effective behavior,* never succumbing to the ease of allowing or excusing anything less. Always stretching yourself to maximize your performance. To want something is one thing; to *will* it is quite another. A relentless will is the hallmark of the elite competitor. Giving in is unacceptable to him. During competition, concede nothing. Ever.

What you should want from yourself is well expressed by the writer Bryce Courtenay: "The power never to compromise…[to] have the fortitude…the guts!…the stamina for the long haul."

RESPONSIBILITY

The American Heritage Dictionary defines **responsibility** as "a duty, obligation, or burden." The more responsible a hitter feels — for whatever result and for whatever reason — the greater the "burden" will be. Too great, then, for that perceived responsibility to be adequately met.

Former Braves outfielder Dale Murphy was — and is — a very responsible person. The key, as a hitter, is to be responsible for yourself. You can't carry others on your back. Such a burden slows your swing down, and the perspective clouds your vision in the batter's box. Murphy tried to carry a poor Braves team. His performance was remarkable, but it would have been better without the burden. His body would have been free to express the great talent he had. Two MVP's still didn't indicate how good he was.

More recently, Florida Marlins outfielder Mark Kotsay was having a very particular problem as a hitter. He was "a third out" with men in scoring position and two outs. [See Chapter 5] He felt so responsible for knocking in runs with two out and runners in scoring position that he focused on that result, rather than on the process.

"You relax, see the ball, and look for a ball you can drive early in the count," I had told him.

Simple to say; difficult to remember — when your mind is focused on responsibility and result, rather than how you want to behave. Keep your thinking small, instead of dragging the burden of responsibility up to the batter's box — and having it weigh you down.

You have a good chance of getting the right result if you enact the right approach. *That's* a responsibility you have control over.

SLUMPS

I don't like the word. The reason I don't like it is that hitters, fans, friends, family, and media-types don't usually define it appropriately. They believe that not getting hits constitutes a slump. It doesn't. A player may be doing everything right at the plate, but he doesn't get the results. Line drives are hit at defensive players, great plays are made in the gaps, and so on. Stay with it.

But players often do not stay with it — "it" being the good approach they've had during those tough-luck at-bats. So they start to press. Their muscles tighten; the bat comes through the hitting zone slower; they change their stance; they think about mechanics and don't see the ball well because of that distraction in the box.

Here are some other reasons players have given me when the say they're "messed up" and in a slump.

A) They're trying to hold on to their batting average. *Result:* divided attention; poor looks at the ball; tight muscles and slow bat through the hitting zone.

KNOW ZONE

B) "I'm swinging at everything." *Result:* over-swinging without discrimination when they have been going well, because they think they can hit everything — or over-swinging out of desperation without seeing anything.

C) Thinking about mechanics in the box. *Result:* the analysis does, indeed, bring on paralysis in the box. He loses the approach of seeing the ball and being easy.

D) "I'm going good and I've got to keep it going." *Result:* disaster follows. Lack of trust, loss of easy swing; all else will break down, as well. *This is very* common — and the irony is clear. A hitter who's "got it going" becomes desperate to *keep it going*, forgetting that what he's got going is his **good approach**. He forgets that and starts thinking about his **results.**

Players tell me their perceived slump "snowballs out of control." The metaphor I often use is one of a stone falling downward, accelerating at a rate of 32 feet per second, squared. All of the aforementioned behaviors send the hitter hurtling into the abyss of a "slump."

Whether size or speed becomes the metaphor, the actuality is a loss of control. The hitter's approach has broken down — and *that is* a slump: a loss of ability to control your approach to what you want to happen and your response to what does happen.

The result cannot ever be controlled, so why should results be considered as indicators of a "slump"? They wouldn't be — if the hitter had a healthy understanding of his game and responsibility.

See the ball; be aggressive; be under control; relax — and hit it hard somewhere. If you're doing that, you're not in a slump. If you stop doing that, you'll be in one before very long. [Re-read Chapter 11]

STRIKEOUTS

This topic, believe it or not, is one of the most talked about by hitters during my years dealing with them. So I will give it the time it demands — not deserves.

A good place to start is with a question posed to Cleveland first baseman Jim Thome — and his response. Question: Should you try to cut down your strikeouts? Answer: "No. You should try to play your game. And if that means striking out, then so be it."

But you don't "play your game" without regard to what's going on in and around you. Learning means improving your game. And so in that regard, Thome's point of view is supportable because you do not dwell on what's wrong with your game, but you can learn strategies that help you improve it. Focus on the positive; focus on positive function — what you can do — or should!

For example, Dale Murphy, after the season for which he was given his first MVP Award, decided he would go to the Braves Instructional League program for a couple of weeks. He told me this during a phone conversation. "What is your reason for going?" I asked. "What's your goal?"

He responded: "I want to learn how to hit that slider down and away."

I suggested that it might be a better idea "to learn how *to lay off* the slider down and away." To be more selective and discriminating about what pitches he swings at. The point was obvious to Murphy, of course — once he came at it from the point of view of how to make good contact, rather than how to avoid striking out so much. One is accomplished when the other is. But neither is accomplished if the point of approach is from what one doesn't want to happen. Both can be accomplished if the focus is on what one wants to happen.

One clarification here: the phone conversation might indicate to the reader that Murphy's "hitting the ball down and away" is a positive, functional goal. In fact, it is. And that my advice that he "lay off the slider down and away" seems to be negative. It can be.

But in the hitter's actual approach to hitting (self-talk) he will tell himself what he is looking for (a ball in a specific location), rather than what he's not looking for. Or what he's afraid he can't handle. So the actual functional command is always direct, positive, and functional. Preliminary talk about a problem or situation can be more free-wheeling without harm being done. *The issue in the batter's box is not avoiding a strikeout, but making good contact.*

It isn't true that coaches and managers fail to be philosophical or understanding when regarding hitters' strikeouts. In

August 2000, Marlins outfielder Preston Wilson led the league with 156 strikeouts. *He* wasn't concerned, and his manager John Boles didn't seem to be either.

Said Boles, when asked about Wilson's strikeouts, "They don't concern me, because he is still learning and developing. As long as he stays productive and keeps driving in runs, we can live with the strikeouts."

Wilson became the 23rd player in history to compile a 30-30 season (home runs and stolen bases).

The point is — an issue wasn't made of the strikeouts. If you go to the plate "trying not to strike out," you're in trouble as soon as you bring that thought into the batter's box. Learn and develop, as Boles said. Think about solutions, rather than problems. Strategies, rather than fears.

THINKING TOO MUCH

This topic has actually been addressed in an earlier context. [See Chapter 5 Self-Talk] But it's a phrase so frequently heard and used by hitters that I felt it deserved a final reference. To reiterate, the problem is not in the thinking itself, it is in the quality, timing, and tonality of the thoughts. In the hitter's box, it should be, "See the ball; be easy." That *is* thinking, but it's *appropriate* thinking.

Item: Mets third baseman Robin Ventura — a good hitter — struggled during the 2000 season. Simply put, by Tom Robson, his hitting coach that season, it was a matter of "over-thinking at the plate." Another way of saying "thinking too much."

Item: Torontos outfielder Jose Cruz got off to a rare good start during the 2000 season. His explanation was that he had a plan that required patience and eliminated confusion — thinking too much. "I don't feel like I have a million things going through my mind," Cruz explained. "Things are so much easier because there's less to think about."

Any such expression indicates that a hitter's mind had been cluttered and his muscles became tight. What he's "over-thinking" about, only he knows, unless he shares his thought(s). What he *isn't* thinking should be clear to everyone. He is not thinking about seeing the ball well.

That's enough for a hitter to have in his head as the pitcher delivers the ball.

TOUGH OUT

It's high praise for a hitter to be called a "tough out." What the speaker is suggesting is that this guy doesn't give an at-bat away. That the at-bat must be won from him. That <u>he concedes nothing to the pitcher.</u> That this guy forces the pitcher to work — to get deep into the count and to have difficulty closing the at-bat.

A hitter such as this is able to <u>discipline himself so as to lay off "a pitcher's strike" early in the count, meaning a pitch that, though in the strike zone, is not in the preferred hitting</u> zone. A hitter such as this fouls off tough pitches with two strikes on him. He forces the pitcher's pitch count to rise. He forces the pitcher to expend physical and mental energy.

As I write this, a number of current players come to mind, but the name that jumps into my head is one that's probably entirely unfamiliar to young readers. The name is Luke Appling, who was a marvel. He had the ability to foul off pitch after pitch when he had two strikes on him. I saw Appling play when I was a youngster going to games at Yankee Stadium. I sensed he was a tough out before I knew there *was* such a description.

His nickname was "Old Aches and Pains." But he was tough enough to play 20 years — all with the Chicago White Sox — from 1930 to 1950. His lifetime batting average was .310. He walked 1,302 times and had 8,857 officials career at-bats. That's 10,159 plate appearances. (No sacrifice fly in those days.) He struck out only 512 times. A real tough out.

TRYING

George Brett talking about hitting .400. "I was having fun with it," he said. But as the season got into August, he kept hearing about it, seemingly from everyone. "It got to me. I started trying to hit .400 and it was all over." He hit .390; the year was 1980.

In September 2000, the New York Mets were struggling to win games in their quest to win the National League East. Catcher

Mike Piazza had a good game in a win against the Reds. After the game, Piazza assessed the recent problems.

"It's obvious we're pressing as a team," he said. "We're just trying too hard. We're taking bad swings and helping pitchers out, and that's it."

Bobby Bonilla had hit seven home runs during spring training in 1997. At the beginning of that championship season for the Marlins, Bonilla struggled. He approached me, telling me how he had hit those homers before the real season and how he had *none* — and it was almost May.

"Are you trying to hit it out?" I asked. He nodded his head, affirming he was indeed trying.

"Were you trying to hit homers during spring training?" The expression of understanding on his face indicated his answer to the question. The right approach often hides behind clouds of intense need. The clouds parted; he remembered how to get what he wanted.

Note: First baseman Tino Martinez had been going through a difficult time with his hitting during the Yankees' 2000 season. On September 24 he *raised* his batting average to .256, hitting two home runs in the game that night.

Said Martinez after the game, "It's been tough all year, not just this recent slump. I think I was trying too hard to hit home runs, and I just didn't have the right approach."

All of the approaches above created tension in mind and muscle. The intent was inappropriate, the focus was misdirected, the muscles were tight. The bat dragged through the hitting zone.

Let me here refer again to Dr. Laurence Morehouse's *Maximum Performance.* In this oft-quoted section, he emphasizes the negative effects of tension created by trying too hard. I quote it, in hopes of provoking the reader to consider, then, what the positive effects will be: *freedom* of mind and muscle from the urgency implicit in "trying hard" to perform a physical act. Says Morehouse:

"When you are putting all you have got into an action, some of that force is holding you back. Muscles are grouped around joints in such a way as to oppose each other. While one group acts as accelerators, another acts as brakes. The muscles acting as brakes stabilize the limbs while accelerating muscles move them...

"Ideally, both braking and accelerating muscles act in harmony to make movement smooth and accurate. In order to move at your best, one system must be releasing while the other is hauling. *You must feel like you are functioning with only a modest amount of power and effort.* [My emphasis.] In rapid movement it is not the strength of the muscle that is important so much as the ability to relax the antagonistic muscles."

Be easy and trust it will happen when the approach is right because your talent then has a chance to express itself: to be *free*. Remind yourself always: trust, rather than try. Then there will be enough pressure internally to withstand whatever is there externally.

WALKS

Bases on balls. Effective hitters know the value of a walk. [Refer again to Chapter 2, where this subject is treated in a broader context.]

Item: From the September 25, 2000 issue of *The Sporting News* — "Part of the reason for the abysmal play [of the Tampa Bay Devil Rays] this month is the team's amazing inability to draw a walk. Tampa Bay even went four games without drawing a walk — the longest stretch in the A.L. since 1992. It was yet another sign of a team in a funk and pressing too hard to snap out of it. No one has been selective at the plate."

Contrast that with the Yankees of recent years, with the Oakland Athletics, in general, and their 2000 MVP, Jason Giambi, in particular.

Those individuals who do not see the ball well — and who are not patient and/or under control are failing to enact the prerequisites for effective performance as a hitter. Walks make hitters better not because of a base gained, but because of an approach maintained.

X-FACTOR

I tell young hitters that the X-factor in their careers is their **belief** in themselves as players. "One man with a belief is worth 99 with an opinion," I say to them.

Mike Bordick was an undrafted shortstop out of the University of Maine. When he was playing for Oakland's Class-A team, a scout from another organization pointed at him and said to me, "That's the kind of kid who'll never get out of A ball." Another opinion. Bordick believed otherwise. The proof was in the belief the player had, not the opinion held by the scout. So it should be.

Well-intentioned coaches and instructors and managers have opinions about how a hitter should go about his task. But in the final analysis, the player must believe in what he is doing. He can listen to everyone, but he must act upon his own trust in himself and his approach.

It's very important to remind yourself that it's more difficult for a pitcher to challenge a hitter who believes in himself than it is for him to pitch effectively to someone who does not. Believe in your preparation; believe in your approach; trust your talent. By doing so, you give yourself the best chance to succeed.

I remember a line Walt Weiss used years ago: "If you want a guarantee, go buy a toaster." There is no guarantee or magic being presented here. But effort is within your control. Your attitude is within your control. An effective approach is within your control. Outcome is not. So your belief is *not* based on the idea that you'll get everything you want — but, rather, that you'll *do* everything necessary in striving for it. *That* you can believe in — if, in fact, you are doing it!

Writer Bryce Courtenay, again: "Only a sustained and invincible belief in yourself will allow you to maintain your integrity and achieve the goals you have set for yourself..."

Tug McGraw of the 1969 Miracle Mets was more succinct: "You gotta believe."

And consider the words of an ancient sage, who said, "Believing is more perceptive than seeing."

My own final *after-words*: Believe in yourself — **and see the ball!**

About the Author

Harvey A. Dorfman's background has been in education as a teacher, counselor, coach, and consultant. He has a Master's Degree in Communications/Psychology and is most knowledgeable about baseball and the factors necessary for success in the game. He was employed from 1984 through 1993 as the Oakland A's full-time instructor/counselor and from 1994 through 1997 with the Florida Marlins. He joined the Tampa Bay Devil Rays in the same capacity in 1998. In 1999 Dorfman became a full-time sport psychology consultant for the Scott Boras Corporation. He lectures extensively on sports psychology, management and leadership training, and personal development. He has, as well, been a consultant to the Vancouver Canucks and the New York Islanders of the NHL, and to a number of major universities. In addition he has experience as a newspaper columnist and freelance journalist, writing for *The New York Times*, *Boston Globe*, and *Miami Herald*, among others. In 1989, his first book, *The Mental Game of Baseball: A Guide to Peak Performance*, co-authored with Karl Kuehl, was released. Published by Diamond Communications, Inc., this bestselling book is considered to be the classic guide to developing the mental mechanics of the game. In 2000, Dorfman's *The Mental ABC's of Pitching: A Handbook for Performance Enhancement* was released, also by Diamond Communications, Inc.